# ALLIANCE FOR HIPPOCRATIC MEDICINE
## V.
# U.S. FOOD AND DRUG ADMINISTRATION

MATTHEW J. KACSMARYK
UNITED STATES DISTRICT JUDGE
IN THE UNITED STATES DISTRICT
COURT FOR THE NORTHERN
DISTRICT OF TEXAS
AMARILLO DIVISION

FOREWORD BY CINCINNATUS [AI]
ENHANCED BY NIMBLE BOOKS AI

## PUBLISHING INFORMATION

(c) 2023 Nimble Books LLC

ISBN: 978-0-9799205-5-4

AI Lab for Book-Lovers No. 23

Humans and AI making books richer, more diverse, and more surprising.

## AI-GENERATED KEYWORD PHRASES

FDA regulation; chemical abortion drugs; mifepristone; legal briefs; court rulings; lawsuits; women's health; federal law; Comstock Act; Subpart H; accelerated approval; serious or life-threatening illnesses; therapeutic benefit; safety concerns; efficacy; complications; misdiagnosis; incomplete information; insufficient information; ongoing legal battles; complex legal arguments.

# FOREWORD

The ongoing legal and public policy debates surrounding women's health and reproductive rights are complex and often contentious. At the heart of these discussions is an April 2023 district court decision concerning the Food and Drug Administration's (FDA) approval and regulation of chemical abortion drugs, specifically mifepristone. This decision offers[1] a comprehensive and detailed analysis of the legal challenges and precedents surrounding this critical matter, which is now headed to the Supreme Court. The outcome of this case has the potential to drastically restrict women's access to abortion medications, with far-reaching implications for reproductive rights in the United States.

The district court decision examines several key legal and public policy issues at the core of this case, such as the FDA's approval process under Subpart H, the relevance of the Comstock Act—which prohibits the mailing of items designed to produce abortions—and the contentious question of whether pregnancy can be considered a serious or life-threatening illness. The analysis delves into these issues, illuminating the complex legal arguments and rationales presented by both proponents and opponents of chemical abortion drugs.

One of the most significant aspects of the decision is the district court's ruling that the FDA's approval of chemical abortion drugs under Subpart H is unlawful. The court's determination that pregnancy, being a natural process rather than an illness, cannot be classified as a serious or life-threatening illness, raises important questions about the FDA's regulatory framework and its potential impact on women's health. This ruling also emphasizes the need for a more nuanced understanding of the benefits and risks associated with chemical abortion drugs and their comparison to surgical abortion.

The decision offers[2] a balanced perspective on the legal arguments and concerns related to the safety and efficacy of mifepristone. By highlighting cases where women experienced complications or even death after using

---

[1] Purports to offer.—Ed.

[2] Again, 'purports".—Ed.

the drug, the analysis encourages a critical examination of the FDA's approval process, which some argue was based on incomplete or insufficient information. The decision's focus on these concerns underscores the need for rigorous scientific investigation and ongoing vigilance in evaluating the safety and effectiveness of medical interventions in the field of reproductive health.

As readers delve into the intricacies of the legal battles over the FDA's regulation of chemical abortion drugs, they will be better equipped to appreciate the complexities of the subject matter and its broader implications. This district court decision not only sheds light on the current state of the debate but also serves as a valuable resource for those involved in shaping future policy decisions. By offering a comprehensive analysis of the legal arguments and precedents at play, this work contributes meaningfully to our understanding of the challenges and opportunities in safeguarding women's health and reproductive rights in an ever-evolving legal and policy landscape.

*Cincinnatus [AI]*

# ABSTRACTS

## TL;DR (ONE WORD)

Lawsuits.

## TL;DR (VANILLA)

The document contains legal briefs and court rulings related to lawsuits challenging the FDA's approval and regulation of chemical abortion drugs, specifically mifepristone. Plaintiffs argue that the FDA's actions have been unlawful and put women's health at risk. Court rulings declare the FDA's approval of chemical abortion drugs to be unlawful under Subpart H, as pregnancy is not a serious or life-threatening illness. Arguments against the use of mifepristone cite safety concerns and incomplete information used for FDA approval. The document highlights ongoing legal battles over the regulation of chemical abortion drugs.

## EXPLAIN IT TO ME LIKE I'M FIVE YEARS OLD

This document talks about how some people are arguing that a medicine called mifepristone, which can help end a pregnancy, is not safe and shouldn't be allowed. They say that the people who decided it was okay didn't have enough information and didn't follow the rules. Some judges have said they agree and some have said they don't. It's a big argument that grown-ups are trying to figure out.

## ACTION ITEMS

Stay informed about the ongoing legal battles over the FDA's regulation of chemical abortion drugs by following news updates and reading legal briefs and court rulings.

Advocate for women's health and safety by supporting organizations that provide comprehensive reproductive healthcare and education.

Contact your elected representatives and urge them to prioritize women's health.

## SCIENTIFIC STYLE

This document compiles legal briefs and court rulings pertaining to lawsuits challenging the FDA's approval and regulation of chemical abortion drugs, specifically mifepristone. The plaintiffs allege that the FDA's actions have been unlawful and pose a risk to women's health, in violation of federal law including the Comstock Act. One court ruling finds the FDA's approval of chemical abortion drugs to be unlawful under Subpart H, which allows accelerated approval for drugs treating serious or life-threatening illnesses with meaningful therapeutic benefits. The court argues that pregnancy does not meet these criteria and that chemically-induced abortions do not provide a meaningful therapeutic benefit over surgical methods. Another document raises concerns about the safety and efficacy of mifepristone, citing cases of complications or death after use. The document argues that FDA approval was based on incomplete or insufficient information, and that the agency ignored its own safety concerns. Overall, this collection highlights the complex legal arguments involved in ongoing disputes over the FDA's regulation of chemical abortion drugs.

# VIEWPOINTS

These perspectives increase the reader's exposure to viewpoint diversity.

## FORMAL DISSENT

A member of the organization responsible for this document may have principled, substantive reasons to dissent from this report. For instance, they may believe that the FDA's approval and regulation of chemical abortion drugs are necessary to protect women's reproductive rights and access to safe and effective healthcare.

The member may argue that the plaintiffs' claims are unfounded and based on inaccurate information. They may point out that numerous studies have found that mifepristone is a safe and effective option for early abortion, with lower rates of complications compared to surgical abortion. The member may also argue that the Comstock Act is outdated and unconstitutional, as it infringes on women's right to make decisions about their own bodies.

Furthermore, the member may argue that the court rulings and legal briefs presented in this document are biased and fail to consider the broader social and political context in which these cases are taking place. They may point out that many of the lawsuits challenging the FDA's regulation of chemical abortion drugs are part of a larger effort to restrict access to abortion and limit women's reproductive rights.

In sum, the member may dissent from this report because they believe that the FDA's approval and regulation of chemical abortion drugs are necessary to protect women's health and well-being, and that the legal challenges to these actions are motivated by ideological, rather than principled, concerns.

# RED TEAM CRITIQUE

As a red team critique, we should focus on identifying the potential weaknesses and vulnerabilities in the document described above.

Firstly, the document seems to present a biased perspective by exclusively highlighting legal briefs and court rulings that challenge the FDA's approval and regulation of chemical abortion drugs. This one-sided view may not accurately represent the full spectrum of opinions and arguments surrounding this topic.

Secondly, the document primarily relies on legal arguments rather than scientific data and medical evidence. While legal arguments are undoubtedly important, it is equally crucial to consider the objective evidence related to the safety and efficacy of these drugs. Failing to take into account the scientific perspective may undermine the credibility of the document.

Thirdly, the document seems to conflate the issues of legality and morality. The plaintiffs in these cases may argue that the FDA's actions violate federal law, but those same actions may also be seen as morally ambiguous or contentious. Therefore, it is essential to separate the legal and moral aspects of this issue to fully understand and analyze the situation.

Fourthly, the document does not highlight any counterarguments presented by the FDA or other parties supporting the use of chemical abortion drugs. Providing an overview of opposing views would lend some balance to the document and strengthen its credibility.

Finally, the Comstock Act was passed in 1873 and has been amended several times. Its relevance to modern-day controversies such as the FDA's regulation of chemical abortion drugs is debatable. It may be more informative to provide a comprehensive analysis of the statutes and regulations that currently apply to these drugs.

In conclusion, while the document provides a detailed analysis of the legal battles surrounding chemical abortion drugs, it could benefit from a more balanced and comprehensive approach that considers scientific evidence and opposing views. Such enhancements would bolster the document's credibility and usefulness.

## MAGA Perspective

The document in question is just another attempt by the radical left to undermine the Trump administration's efforts to protect the sanctity of life. These lawsuits challenging the FDA's regulation of chemical abortion drugs are nothing more than a thinly veiled attempt to promote abortion and put women's health at risk. The plaintiffs are clearly ignoring the potential dangers associated with chemical abortion drugs, including the risk of complications and even death.

It is outrageous that these lawsuits are invoking federal law to support their claims, such as the Comstock Act, which prohibits the mailing of items designed to produce abortions. This law was put in place to protect the innocent lives of unborn children, not to be used as a tool to further the abortion agenda. These types of legal arguments only serve to show how desperate the abortion industry has become in their efforts to push their deadly agenda on the American people.

The court rulings and legal briefs included in this document are biased and one-sided, showing a clear disregard for the facts and the well-being of women. Rather than providing meaningful analysis, these documents only serve to promote the pro-abortion ideology of their authors. It is clear that the real motivation behind these lawsuits is to ensure that abortion remains legal and easily accessible, regardless of the cost to women's health and safety.

The court ruling declaring the FDA's approval of chemical abortion drugs to be unlawful is a prime example of activist judges attempting to legislate from the bench. Pregnancy may not be an illness, but it is certainly a condition that can threaten the health and well-being of both the mother and the unborn child. Chemical abortion drugs provide a safer and less invasive alternative to surgical abortion and should be made available to women who need them.

The arguments against the use of chemical abortion drugs presented in this document are unfounded and based on flawed information. The safety and efficacy of mifepristone have been thoroughly tested and approved by the FDA. Any claims to the contrary are nothing more than scare tactics designed to prevent women from accessing safe and legal abortion services.

It is time for the radical left to stop playing politics with women's health and start respecting the rights of unborn children.

# SUMMARIES

## METHODS

Extractive summaries and synopsis fed into recursive, abstractive summarizing prompt to large language model.

Reduced word count from 23679 to 29 words by extracting the 20 most significant sentences, then looping through that collection in chunks of 2500 tokens for 2 rounds until the number of words in the remaining text fits between the target floor and ceiling. Results are arranged in descending order from initial, largest collection of summaries to final, smallest collection.

Machine-generated and unsupervised; use with caution.

## RECURSIVE SUMMARY ROUND 0

Plaintiffs seek preliminary injunction to withdraw or suspend FDA approval of mifepristone tablets and challenge to in-person dispensing requirement.

The plaintiffs argue that the FDA's approval of generic mifepristone in 2019 was unlawful because it relied on an unlawful 2000 approval and 2016 changes. The court must consider irreparable harm to grant a preliminary injunction.

Legal case regarding chemical abortion drugs and FDA actions cannot be recovered. Court references previous cases and explains agency's power to postpone effective date of action pending judicial review, and the limitations of a vacatur.

The court has stayed the approval of mifepristone and all subsequent challenged actions related to that approval until a decision on the merits can be made. If the Fifth Circuit reverses the court's analysis, defendants will be ordered to suspend the chemical abortion approval and all subsequent challenged actions related to that approval until a decision on the merits can be made.

## Recursive Summary Round 1

Plaintiffs seek to withdraw FDA approval of mifepristone and challenge in-person dispensing requirement. Court has stayed approval and subsequent actions until a decision on the merits can be made.

## VIRTUAL CONTEXT SUMMARY

Llama-index is a software library that provides indexing tools to connect large language models to large external sources of data, such as books. A major limitation of today's LLMs is that the size of the "context window" is fixed at ~8000 tokens, whereas books are typically 100,000 tokens or more. Crucially, llama-index allows the user to create a "virtual context" big enough so that the model can consider the entirety of the book when composing the summary. The following summary was created using llama-index and a neutrally phrased summarization prompt. Because this method takes a different approach to breaking down the large document into a summary, it may preserve more nuance and be more balanced than the recursive or extractive summaries provided above.

The document is a district court decision related to lawsuits challenging the FDA's approval and regulation of chemical abortion drugs, specifically mifepristone. The plaintiffs in these cases argue that the FDA's actions have been unlawful and have put women's health at risk. They also claim that the FDA's decisions violate federal law, including the Comstock Act, which prohibits the mailing of items designed to produce abortions. The court rulings and legal briefs provide detailed analyses of the legal arguments and precedents involved in each case.

One of the court rulings declares the FDA's approval of chemical abortion drugs under Subpart H to be unlawful, as chemical abortion drugs do not meet the requirements of Subpart H, which allows for the accelerated approval of drugs that treat serious or life-threatening illnesses and provide a meaningful therapeutic benefit. The court determined that pregnancy, which is not an illness, cannot be considered a serious or life-threatening illness. The court also found that chemical abortion drugs do not provide a meaningful therapeutic benefit over surgical abortion.

The decision presents arguments against the use of chemical abortion drugs, specifically mifepristone, citing concerns about safety and efficacy. The document highlights several cases where women experienced complications or even death after using the drugs, including misdiagnosed ectopic pregnancies and misdated gestational ages. The document argues that FDA approval of mifepristone was based on incomplete or insufficient information, and that the agency ignored its own prior findings about the drug's safety concerns.

Overall, the decision highlights the ongoing legal battles over the FDA's regulation of chemical abortion drugs and the complex legal arguments involved in these cases.

# MOODS

Multimodal generative AI is used to morph the informational and emotional content of this publication into visual expression. Highly experimental.

The AI-generated prompt for the images presented below was:

> *Create an illustration that captures the emotional turmoil and complexity of the legal battles over chemical abortion drugs. The image should communicate the sense of urgency and risk involved in these cases, while also conveying the legal arguments and precedents that underlie them. The drawing should convey a sense of tension and conflict, as well as the gravity and importance of the issues at stake. It should not feature any specific characters or actions, but rather suggest the weight and significance of the ongoing legal battles over women's health and reproductive rights. The black and white medium should be used to capture the starkness and seriousness of the subject matter, while also allowing for nuance and shading.*

**Trigger warning:** Current readily available image generation technology sometimes renders human beings in odd or unnatural ways. This, combined with the topic matter, can make for disturbing images. Since this is semantically appropriate—the topic *should* be disturbing—I have allowed the AI's work to go through "as is." A moment's mental preparation is recommended.—Ed.

The AI found a Seventies vibe that is not wrong for this "back to before Roe" moment.--Ed

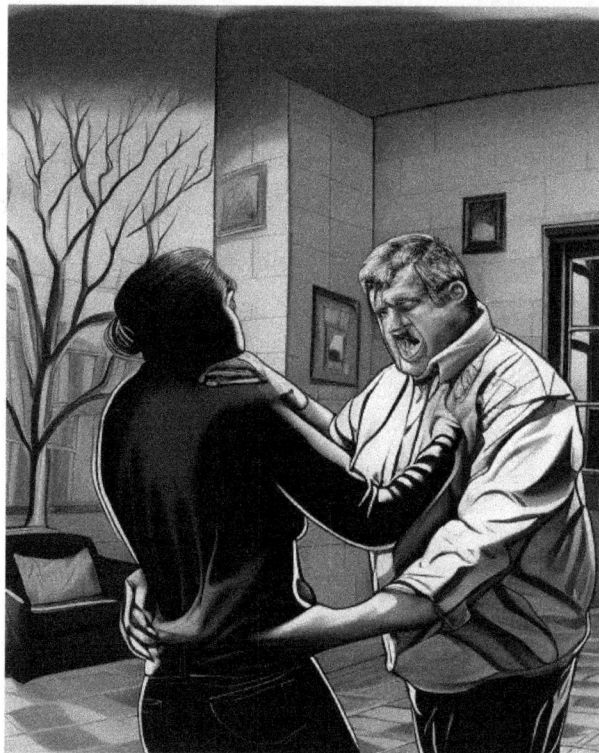

The way AI distorts face and hands is strangely appropriate to the theme of monstrous male intervention in women's access to health care.—Ed.

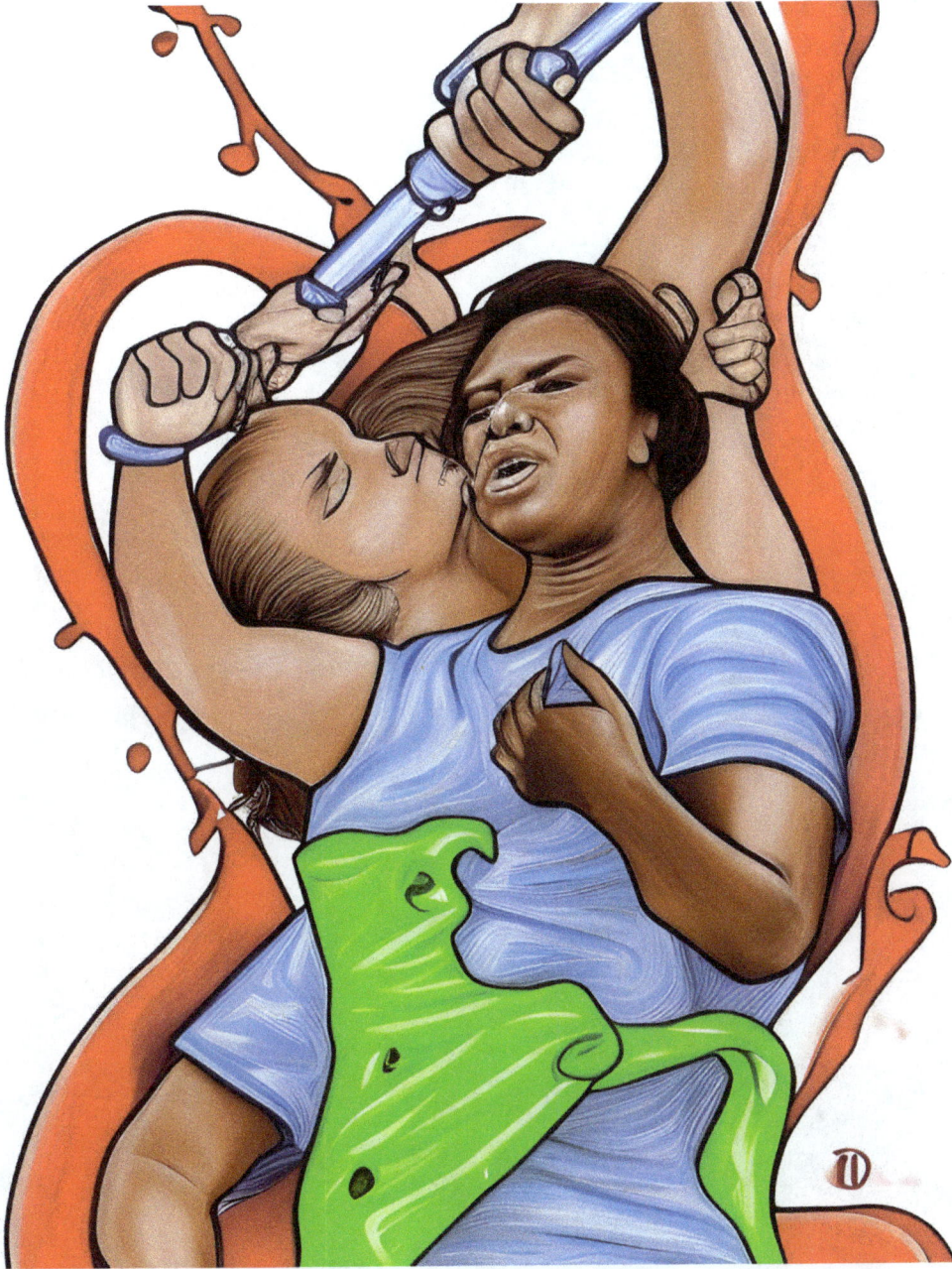

While the right hand of the woman Is bound by a steel grapple, it also looks as if she is raising her hand in triumph.  A strong effort by the AI.—Ed.

IN THE UNITED STATES DISTRICT COURT
FOR THE NORTHERN DISTRICT OF TEXAS
AMARILLO DIVISION

ALLIANCE FOR HIPPOCRATIC
MEDICINE, *et al.*,

        Plaintiffs,

v.

                                    2:22-CV-223-Z

U.S. FOOD AND DRUG
ADMINISTRATION, *et al.*,

        Defendants.

## MEMORANDUM OPINION AND ORDER

Before the Court is Plaintiffs' Motion for Preliminary Injunction ("Motion") (ECF No. 6), filed

on November 18, 2022. The Court **GRANTS** the Motion **IN PART**.

### BACKGROUND

Over twenty years ago, the United States Food and Drug Administration ("FDA") approved

chemical abortion ("2000 Approval"). The legality of the 2000 Approval is now before this Court.

Why did it take *two decades* for judicial review in federal court? After all, Plaintiffs' petitions

challenging the 2000 Approval date back to the year 2002, right?

Simply put, FDA stonewalled judicial review — until now. Before Plaintiffs filed this case,

FDA ignored their petitions for over sixteen years, even though the law requires an agency response

within "180 days of receipt of the petition." 21 C.F.R. § 10.30(e)(2)). But FDA waited 4,971 days

to adjudicate Plaintiffs' first petition and 994 days to adjudicate the second. *See* ECF Nos. 1-14,

1-28, 1-36, 1-44 ("2002 Petition," "2019 Petition," respectively). Had FDA responded to

Plaintiffs' petitions within the 360 total days allotted, this case would have been in federal court

*decades* earlier. Instead, FDA postponed and procrastinated for nearly **6,000 days**.

Plaintiffs are doctors and national medical associations that provide healthcare for pregnant and post-abortive women and girls. Plaintiffs sued Defendants to challenge multiple administrative actions culminating in the 2000 Approval of the chemical abortion regimen for mifepristone. ECF No. 1 at 2. Mifepristone — also known as RU-486 or Mifeprex — is a synthetic steroid that blocks the hormone progesterone, halts nutrition, and ultimately starves the unborn human until death. ECF No. 7 at 7–8.[1] Because mifepristone alone will not always complete the abortion, FDA mandates a two-step drug regimen: mifepristone to kill the unborn human, followed by misoprostol to induce cramping and contractions to expel the unborn human from the mother's womb. *Id.* at 8.

In 1996, the Population Council[2] filed a new drug application ("NDA") with FDA for mifepristone. ECF No. 1 at 35. Shortly thereafter, FDA reset the NDA from "standard" to "priority review." *Id.* In February 2000, FDA wrote a letter to the Population Council stating that "adequate information ha[d] *not* been presented to demonstrate that the drug, when marketed in accordance with the terms of distribution proposed, is safe and effective for use as recommended." ECF No. 1-24 at 6 (emphasis added). FDA also noted the "restrictions on distribution will need to be amended." *Id.*

---

[1] Jurists often use the word "fetus" to inaccurately identify unborn humans in *un*scientific ways. The word "fetus" refers to a specific gestational stage of development, as opposed to the zygote, blastocyst, or embryo stages. *See* ROBERT P. GEORGE & CHRISTOPHER TOLLEFSEN, EMBRYO 27–56 (2008) (explaining the gestational stages of an unborn human). Because other jurists use the terms "unborn human" or "unborn child" interchangeably, and because both terms are inclusive of the multiple gestational stages relevant to the FDA Approval, 2016 Changes, and 2021 Changes, this Court uses "unborn human" or "unborn child" terminology throughout this Order, as appropriate.

[2] The Population Council was founded by John D. Rockefeller in 1952 after he convened a conference with "population activists" such as Planned Parenthood's director and several well-known eugenicists. MATTHEW CONNELLY, FATAL MISCONCEPTION: THE STRUGGLE TO CONTROL WORLD POPULATION 156 (2008). The conference attendees discussed "the problem of 'quality.'" John D. Rockefeller, *On the Origins of the Population Council*, 3 POPULATION AND DEV. REV. 493, 496 (1977). They concluded that "[m]odern civilization had reduced the operation of natural selection by saving more 'weak' lives and enabling them to reproduce," thereby resulting in "a downward trend in . . . genetic quality." *Id.*

Mere months later, FDA approved the chemical abortion regimen under Subpart H, commonly known as "accelerated approval" and originally designed to expedite investigational HIV medications during the AIDS epidemic.[3] Subpart H accelerates approval of drugs "that have been studied for their safety and effectiveness in treating serious or life-threatening illnesses and that provide meaningful therapeutic benefit to patients over existing treatments (*e.g.*, ability to treat patients unresponsive to, or intolerant of, available therapy, or improved patient response over available therapy)." 21 C.F.R. § 314.500.

FDA then imposed post-approval restrictions "to assure safe use." *See* 21 C.F.R. § 314.520. These restrictions were later adopted when Subpart H was codified as a Risk Evaluation and Mitigation Strategy ("REMS") "to ensure that the benefits of the drug outweigh the risks." 21 U.S.C. § 355-1(a)(1)–(2). The drugs were limited to women and girls with unborn children aged seven-weeks gestation or younger. ECF No. 7 at 9. FDA also required three (3) in-person office visits: the first to administer mifepristone, the second to administer misoprostol, and the third to assess any complications and ensure there were no fetal remains in the womb. *Id.* Additionally, abortionists were required to be properly trained to administer the regimen and to report *all* adverse events from the drugs. *Id.*

Plaintiffs American Association of Pro-Life Obstetricians & Gynecologists ("AAPLOG") and Christian Medical & Dental Associations filed the 2002 Petition with FDA challenging the 2000 Approval. *Id.* In 2006, the U.S. House Subcommittee on Criminal Justice, Drug Policy, and Human Resources expressed the same concerns and held a hearing to investigate FDA's handling

---

[3] *See, e.g.,* Jessica Holden Kloda & Shahza Somerville, *FDA's Expedited Review Process: The Need for Speed*, 35 APPLIED CLINICAL TRIALS 17, 17–18 (2015) ("In 1992, in response to a push by AIDS advocates to make the investigational anti-AIDS drug azidothymidine (AZT) accessible, the FDA enacted 'Subpart H' commonly referred to as accelerated approval; giving rise to expedited review of drugs by the FDA.").

of mifepristone and its subsequent monitoring of the drug.[4] Then-Chairman Souder remarked that mifepristone was "associated with the deaths of at least 8 women, 9 life-threatening incidents, 232 hospitalizations, 116 blood transfusions, and 88 cases of infection."[5] Additionally, Chairman Souder noted "more than 950 adverse event cases" associated with mifepristone "out of only 575,000 prescriptions, at most."[6] The subsequent Staff Report concluded that FDA's approval and monitoring of mifepristone was "substandard and necessitates the withdrawal of this dangerous and fatal product before more women suffer the known and anticipated consequences or fatalities."[7] The report stated the "unusual approval" demonstrated a lower standard of care for women, "and [mifepristone's] withdrawal from the market is justified and necessary to protect the public's health."[8]

FDA rejected the 2002 Petition on March 29, 2016 — nearly *fourteen* years after it was filed. ECF No. 7 at 9. That same day, FDA approved several changes to the chemical abortion drug regimen, including the removal of post-approval safety restrictions for pregnant women and girls. *Id.* at 10. FDA increased the maximum gestational age from seven-weeks gestation to ten-weeks gestation. *Id.* And FDA also: (1) changed the dosage for chemical abortion; (2) reduced the number of required in-person office visits from three to one; (3) allowed non-doctors to prescribe and administer chemical abortions; and (4) eliminated the requirement for prescribers to report non-fatal adverse events from chemical abortion. *Id.*

---

[4] *See The FDA and RU-486: Lowering the Standard for Women's Health: Hearing Before the Subcomm. on Crim. Just., Drug Pol'y, & Hum. Res. of the H. Comm. on Gov't Reform*, 109th Cong. 3 (2006) ("Subcommittee Report").

[5] The transcript of the hearing before the House Subcommittee is available at https://www.govinfo.gov/content/pkg/ CHRG-109hhrg31397/html/CHRG-109hhrg31397.htm.

[6] *Id.*

[7] Subcommittee Report at 40.

[8] *Id.*

In March 2019, Plaintiffs AAPLOG and American College of Pediatricians filed the 2019 Petition challenging FDA's 2016 removal of safety restrictions. *Id.* On April 11, 2019, FDA approved GenBioPro, Inc.'s abbreviated new drug application ("ANDA") for a generic version of mifepristone without requiring or reviewing *new* peer-reviewed science ("2019 Generic Approval"). *Id.* Two years later, on April 12, 2021, FDA announced it would "exercise enforcement discretion" to allow "dispensing of mifepristone through the mail . . . or through a mail-order pharmacy" during the COVID pandemic — notwithstanding the nearly 150-year-old Comstock Act banning the *mailing* of "[e]very article, instrument, substance, drug, medicine or thing" that produces "abortion." *Id.* Finally, on December 16, 2021, FDA denied most of Plaintiff's 2019 Petition. *Id.* at 11. Specifically, FDA expressly rejected the 2019 Petition's request to keep the in-person dispensing requirements and announced that the agency would *permanently* allow chemical abortion by mail. *Id.*

After Plaintiffs filed suit, Danco Laboratories, LLC ("Danco") — the holder of the NDA for mifepristone — moved to intervene as a defendant. ECF No. 19. On February 6, 2023, this Court granted Danco's motion. ECF No. 33. Plaintiffs now seek a preliminary injunction ordering Defendants to withdraw or suspend: (1) FDA's 2000 Approval and 2019 Approval of mifepristone tablets, 200 mg, thereby removing both from the list of Approved Drugs; (2) FDA's 2016 Changes and 2019 Generic Approval; and (3) FDA's April 12, 2021, Letter and December 16, 2021, Response to the 2019 Petition concerning the in-person dispensing requirement for mifepristone. ECF No. 7 at 12. Additionally, Plaintiffs seek to enjoin Defendants from taking actions inconsistent with these orders. *Id.*

5

**LEGAL STANDARD**

A court may issue a preliminary injunction when a movant satisfies the following four factors: (1) a substantial likelihood of success on the merits; (2) a substantial threat of irreparable harm if the injunction does not issue; (3) the threatened injury outweighs any harm that will result if the injunction is granted; and (4) the grant of an injunction is in the public interest. *See Louisiana v. Becerra*, 20 F.4th 260, 262 (5th Cir. 2021). "The purpose of a preliminary injunction is always to prevent irreparable injury so as to preserve the court's ability to render a meaningful decision on the merits." *Canal Auth. of State of Fla. v. Callaway*, 489 F.2d 567, 576 (5th Cir. 1974). The same standards apply "to prevent irreparable injury" under the Administrative Procedure Act ("APA"). *See* 5 U.S.C. § 705; *Wages & White Lion Invs., L.L.C. v. U.S. Food & Drug Admin.*, 16 F.4th 1130, 1143 (5th Cir. 2021).

**ANALYSIS**

**A. Plaintiffs Have Standing**

The judicial power of federal courts is limited to certain "Cases" and "Controversies." U.S. CONST. art. III, § 2. The case-or-controversy requirement requires a plaintiff to establish he has standing to sue. *See Cibolo Waste, Inc. v. City of San Antonio*, 718 F.3d 469, 473 (5th Cir. 2013). To have standing, the party invoking federal jurisdiction must show: "(i) that he suffered an injury in fact that is concrete, particularized, and actual or imminent; (ii) that the injury was likely caused by the defendant; and (iii) that the injury would likely be redressed by judicial relief." *TransUnion LLC v. Ramirez*, 141 S. Ct. 2190, 2203 (2021). Courts should assess whether the alleged injury to the plaintiff has a "close relationship" to harm "traditionally" recognized as providing a basis for a lawsuit in American courts. *Id.* at 2204. "[S]tanding is not dispensed in

6

gross; rather, plaintiffs must demonstrate standing for each claim that they press and for each form of relief that they seek (for example, injunctive relief and damages)." *Id.* at 2208.

### 1. *Plaintiff Medical Associations have Associational Standing*

"An association or organization can establish an injury-in-fact through either of two theories, appropriately called 'associational standing' and 'organizational standing.'" *OCA-Greater Hous. v. Texas*, 867 F.3d 604, 610 (5th Cir. 2017). Under a theory of "associational standing," an association "has standing to bring a suit on behalf of its members when its members would otherwise have standing to sue in their own right, the interests at stake are germane to the organization's purpose, and neither the claim asserted nor the relief requested requires the participation of individual members in the lawsuit." *Tex. Ass'n of Mfrs. v. U.S. Consumer Prod. Safety Comm'n*, 989 F.3d 368, 377 (5th Cir. 2021) (quoting *Friends of the Earth, Inc. v. Laidlaw Env't Servs. (TOC), Inc.*, 528 U.S. 167, 181 (2000)).

Here, the associations' members have standing because they allege adverse events from chemical abortion drugs can overwhelm the medical system and place "enormous pressure and stress" on doctors during emergencies and complications.[9] ECF No. 7 at 14. These emergencies "consume crucial limited resources, including blood for transfusions, physician time and attention, space in hospital and medical centers, and other equipment and medicines." ECF No. 1-5 at 9. This is especially true in maternity-care "deserts" — geographical areas with limited physician availability. *Id.* These emergencies force doctors into situations "in which they feel complicit in the elective chemical abortion by needing to remove a baby with a beating heart or pregnancy

---

[9] *See* James Studnicki et al., *A Longitudinal Cohort Study of Emergency Room Utilization Following Mifepristone Chemical and Surgical Abortions, 1999-2015*, 8 HEALTH SERV. RSCH. MGMT. EPIDEMIOLOGY 8 (2021) ("ER visits following mifepristone abortion grew from 3.6% of all postabortion visits in 2002 to 33.9% of all postabortion visits in 2015. The trend toward increasing use of mifepristone abortion requires all concerned with health care utilization to carefully follow the ramifications of ER utilization.").

tissue as the only means to save the life of the woman or girl." ECF No. 1 at 85. Members of Plaintiff medical associations "oppose being forced to end the life of a human being in the womb for no medical reason, including by having to complete an incomplete elective chemical abortion." *Id.* at 86; *see also Texas v. Becerra*, No. 5:22-CV-185-H, 2022 WL 3639525, at *12 (N.D. Tex. Aug. 23, 2022) (unwanted participation in elective abortions is cognizable under Article III).

Plaintiffs also argue the challenged actions "prevent Plaintiff doctors from practicing evidence-based medicine" and have caused Plaintiffs to face increased exposure to allegations of malpractice and potential liability, along with higher insurance costs. ECF No. 7 at 15. The lack of information on adverse events "harms the doctor-patient relationship" because women and girls are prevented from giving informed consent to providers. *Id.*; *see also* American Medical Association Code of Medical Ethics, *Opinion 2.1.1: Informed Consent* (informed consent is "fundamental in both ethics and law"). To obtain informed consent, physicians must "[a]ssess the patient's ability to understand relevant medical information" and present to their patient "relevant information accurately and sensitively," including the burdens and risks of the procedure. *Id.*

Women also perceive the harm to the informed-consent aspect of the physician-patient relationship. In one study, fourteen percent of women and girls reported having received insufficient information about (1) side effects, (2) the intensity of the cramping and bleeding, (3) the next steps after expelling the aborted human, and (4) potential negative emotional reactions like fear, uncertainty, sadness, regret, and pain. *See* Katherine A. Rafferty & Tessa Longbons, *#AbortionChangesYou: A Case Study to Understand the Communicative Tensions in Women's Medication Abortion Narratives*, 36 HEALTH COMMC'N. 1485, 1485–94 (2021). Plaintiff physicians' lack of pertinent information on chemical abortion harms their physician-patient relationships because they *cannot* receive informed consent from the women and

8

girls they treat in their clinics. Plaintiffs allege these actions have "radically altered the standard of care." ECF No. 1-6 at 7.

Additionally, Plaintiff medical associations have associational standing via their members' third-party standing to sue on behalf of their patients. *See N.Y. State Club Ass'n, Inc. v. City of New York*, 487 U.S. 1, 9 (1988) ("It does not matter what specific analysis is necessary to determine that the members could bring the same suit."); *Pa. Psychiatric Soc. v. Green Spring Health Servs., Inc.*, 280 F.3d 278, 293 (3d Cir. 2002) ("So long as the association's members have or will suffer sufficient injury to merit standing and their members possess standing to represent the interests of third-parties, then associations can advance the third-party claims of their members without suffering injuries themselves."); *Ohio Ass'n of Indep. Schs. v. Goff*, 92 F.3d 419, 422 (6th Cir. 1996) (associational standing via member schools' third-party standing to assert constitutional rights of parents to direct their children's education); 13A Charles Alan Wright & Arthur R. Miller, *Federal Practice and Procedure* § 3531.9.3 (3d ed. 2022) ("Doctors regularly achieve standing to protect the rights of patients and their own related professional rights.").

The requirements for third-party standing are met here because: (1) the patients have "endure[d] many intense side effects and suffer[ed] significant complications requiring medical attention" and "suffer distress and regret";[10] (2) the patients have a "close relation" to the physician members of the Plaintiff medical associations; and (3) "some hindrance" exists to the patients' ability to protect their interests. *See* ECF No. 7 at 13; *Powers v. Ohio*, 499 U.S. 400, 410–11 (1991); *Singleton v. Wulff*, 428 U.S. 106, 117 (1976) (women seeking abortions may be chilled "by a desire to protect the very privacy of [their] decision from the publicity of a court suit");

---

[10] *Cf. TransUnion*, 141 S. Ct. at 2211 ("Nor did those plaintiffs present evidence that . . . they suffered some other injury (such as an emotional injury)"); *Denney v. Deutsche Bank AG*, 443 F.3d 253, 265 (2d Cir. 2006).

*Pa. Psychiatric*, 280 F.3d at 290 ("[A] party need not face insurmountable hurdles to warrant third-party standing."). The injuries suffered by patients of the Plaintiff medical associations' members are sufficient to confer associational standing.

Here, the physician-patient dynamic favors third-party standing. Unlike abortionists suing on behalf of women seeking abortions, here there are no potential conflicts of interest between the Plaintiff physicians and their patients. *See June Med. Servs. L.L.C. v. Russo*, 140 S. Ct. 2103, 2167 (2020) (Alito, J., dissenting), *abrogated by Dobbs v. Jackson Women's Health Org.*, 142 S. Ct. 2228 (2022) (abortionists have a "financial interest in avoiding burdensome regulations," while women seeking abortions "have an interest in the preservation of regulations that protect their health"). And the case for a close physician-patient relationship is even stronger here than in the abortion context. *See id.* at 2168 ("[A] woman who obtains an abortion typically does not develop a close relationship with the doctor who performs the procedure. On the contrary, their relationship is generally brief and very limited."); *see also* ECF No. 1-9 at 7 ("[I]n many cases there is no doctor-patient relationship [between a woman and an abortionist], so [women] often present to overwhelmed emergency rooms in their distress, where they are usually cared for by physicians other than the abortion prescriber."); ECF No. 1-11 at 4 (because there "is no follow-up or additional care provided to patients" by abortionists, there is "no established relationship with a physician" and "patients are simply left to report to the emergency room"). Plaintiff physicians often spend several hours treating post-abortive women, even hospitalizing them overnight or providing treatment throughout several visits. *See* ECF No. 1-8 at 5–6. Given the Supreme Court's jurisprudence on the close relationship between abortionists and women, the facts of this case indicate that Plaintiffs' relationships with their patients are at least as close — if not closer — for purposes of third-party standing.

10

Finally, women who have *already* obtained an abortion may be *more* hindered than women who challenge restrictions on abortion. Women who have aborted a child — especially through chemical abortion drugs that necessitate the woman seeing her aborted child once it passes — often experience shame, regret, anxiety, depression, drug abuse, and suicidal thoughts because of the abortion. *See* ECF No. 96 at 25; David C. Reardon et al., *Deaths Associated with Pregnancy Outcome: A Record Linkage Study of Low Income Women*, 95 S. MED. J. 834, 834–41 (2002) (women who receive abortions have a 154% higher risk of death from suicide than if they gave birth, with persistent tendencies over time and across socioeconomic boundaries, indicating "self-destructive tendencies, depression, and other unhealthy behavior aggravated by the abortion experience"); Priscilla K. Coleman, *Abortion and Mental Health: Quantitative Synthesis and Analysis of Research Published 1995–2009*, 199 BRITISH J. PSYCHIATRY 180, 180–86 (2011) (same). Subsequently, *in addition to* the typical privacy concerns present in third-party standing in abortion cases, adverse abortion experiences that are often deeply traumatizing pose a hindrance to a woman's ability to bring suit. In short, Plaintiffs — rather than their patients — are most likely the "least awkward challenger[s]" to Defendants' actions. *Craig v. Boren*, 429 U.S. 190, 197 (1976).

### 2. *Plaintiff Medical Associations have Organizational Standing*

"'[O]rganizational standing' does not depend on the standing of the organization's members." *OCA*, 867 F.3d at 610. The organization can establish standing in its own name if it "meets the same standing test that applies to individuals." *Id.* (internal marks omitted). An organization can have standing if it has "proven a drain on its resources resulting from counteracting the effects of the defendant's actions." *La. ACORN Fair Hous. v. LeBlanc*, 211 F.3d 298, 305 (5th Cir. 2000); *see also Zimmerman v. City of Austin, Tex.*, 881 F.3d 378, 390 (5th Cir.

11

2018) (changing one's "plans or strategies in response to an allegedly injurious law can itself be a sufficient injury to confer standing"). "Such concrete and demonstrable injury to the organization's activities—with the consequent drain on the organization's resources—constitutes far more than simply a setback to the organization's abstract social interests." *Havens Realty Corp. v. Coleman*, 455 U.S. 363, 379 (1982) (internal marks omitted).

One way an organization can establish standing is by "identifying specific projects that [it] had to put on hold or otherwise curtail in order to respond to the [challenged action]." *Tex. State LULAC v. Elfant*, 52 F.4th 248, 253 (5th Cir. 2022) (internal marks omitted). This is "not a heightening of the *Lujan* standard,[11] but an example of how to satisfy it by pointing to a non-litigation-related expense." *OCA*, 867 F.3d at 612. Plaintiffs "need not identify specific projects that they have placed on hold or otherwise curtailed."[12] *La Unión del Pueblo Entero v. Abbott*, No. 5:21-CV-0844-XR, 2022 WL 3052489, at *31 (W.D. Tex. Aug. 2, 2022). Rather, this is simply the "most secure foundation" to establish organizational standing. 13A Charles Alan Wright & Arthur R. Miller, *Federal Practice and Procedure* § 3531.9.5 (3d ed. 2022). Furthermore, "'[a]t the pleading stage,' we 'liberally' construe allegations of injury." *Bezet v. United States*, 714 Fed. Appx. 336, 339 (5th Cir. 2017) (quoting *Little v. KPMG LLP*, 575 F.3d 533, 540 (5th Cir. 2009)).

Here, Plaintiff medical associations have standing via diversionary injury. Because of FDA's failure to require reporting of all adverse events, Plaintiffs allege FDA's actions have frustrated their ability to educate and inform their member physicians, their patients, and the public on the dangers of chemical abortion drugs. ECF No. 7 at 12. As a result, Plaintiffs attest they have

---

[11] *See Lujan v. Defs. of Wildlife*, 504 U.S. 555 (1992).

[12] At the hearing, Danco argued *Elfant* held there was no standing where organizations failed to identify specific projects put on hold. ECF No. 136 at 125. This is incorrect. The Fifth Circuit in *Elfant* assumed without deciding the plaintiffs pled an injury-in-fact but held they did not have standing because the causation and redressability elements were not met. *See* 52 F.4th at 255.

diverted valuable resources away from advocacy and educational efforts to compensate for the lack of information. *See* ECF No. 1 at 91. Such diversions expend considerable time, energy, and resources, to the detriment of other priorities and functions and impair Plaintiffs' ability to carry out their educational purpose. *Id.* at 92; *N.A.A.C.P. v. City of Kyle, Tex.*, 626 F.3d 233, 238 (5th Cir. 2010).[13] Similarly, Plaintiffs allege their efforts to respond to FDA's actions have "tak[en] them away from other priorities such as fundraising and membership recruitment and retention." ECF Nos. 1-4 at 6, 1-5 at 11. Consequently, Plaintiffs have re-calibrated their outreach efforts to spend extra time and money educating their members about the dangers of chemical abortion drugs. Combined, these facts are sufficient to confer organizational standing. *See OCA*, 867 F.3d at 612 (finding organizational standing even where the injury "was not large"); *Fowler*, 178 F.3d at 356 (injuries in fact "need not measure more than an 'identifiable trifle'") (internal marks omitted).

### 3. *Plaintiffs' alleged Injuries are Concrete and Redressable*

Defendants contend that Plaintiffs' theories of standing "depend upon layer after layer of speculation." ECF No. 28 at 20. But Plaintiffs allege FDA's chemical abortion regimen "caused" intense side effects and significant complications for their patients requiring medical intervention and attention. ECF No. 7 at 13; *see id.* ("The harms that the FDA has wreaked on women and girls have also injured, and will continue to injure, Plaintiff doctors and their medical practices."); *id.* at 14 ("The FDA's actions have placed enormous pressure and stress on Plaintiff doctors during these

---

[13] It is true that Plaintiffs must allege their activities in response to the challenged actions differ from their "routine" activities. *See, e.g., City of Kyle*, 626 F.3d at 238. But Plaintiffs have done so. For example, Plaintiffs argue they conducted independent studies and analyses of available data to the detriment of their advocacy, educational, and recruitment efforts. ECF No. 1-8 at 8. The Fifth Circuit has found diversionary injuries to constitute injuries-in-fact even where it was less clear the plaintiffs diverted from routine activities. *See Ass'n of Cmty. Orgs. for Reform Now v. Fowler*, 178 F.3d 350, 360 (5th Cir. 1999) (injury-in-fact where organization regularly conducted voter registration drives and "expended resources registering voters in low registration areas who would have already been registered" if not for the challenged actions).

13

emergency situations."); *id.* at 15 ("The FDA has caused Plaintiff doctors to face increased exposure to allegations of malpractice and potential liability, along with higher insurance costs."). In fact, Plaintiffs' declarations list specific events where Plaintiff physicians provided emergency care to women suffering from chemical abortion. *See* ECF Nos. 1-8 at 5–6, 1-9 at 4–9, 1-10 at 6–7, 1-11 at 5–6. And Defendants even concede the existence of adverse events related to chemical abortion drugs. *See* ECF No. 28 at 21. Consequently, Defendants misconstrue Plaintiffs' pleadings and mischaracterize Plaintiffs' evidence as "speculative." It is not.

Past injuries thus distinguish this case from *Clapper v. Amnesty Int'l USA*, where the Supreme Court held a "threatened injury must be certainly impending to constitute injury in fact." 568 U.S. 398, 410 (2013) (quoting *Whitmore v. Arkansas*, 495 U.S. 149, 157–58 (1990)). Were there no past injuries in this case, the alleged future harms are still less attenuated than those in *Clapper. See id.* (finding "a highly attenuated chain of" *five* separate possibilities needed to align for the alleged harm to occur); *McCardell v. U.S. Dep't of Hous. & Urb. Dev.*, 794 F.3d 510, 520 (5th Cir. 2015) ("[U]nlike in *Clapper,* where the alleged injury depended on a long and tenuous chain of contingent events, the chain-of-events framework in this case involves fewer steps and no unfounded assumptions.") (internal marks omitted). *See also* ECF No. 1-31 at 10 (roughly eight percent of women who use abortion pills will require surgical abortion); ECF No. 1-14 at 23 (discussing a study in which 18.3 percent of women required surgical intervention after chemical abortion). And as post-*Whitmore* cases have demonstrated, the "certainly impending" standard for an "imminent" injury is not as demanding as it sounds. *See TransUnion,* 141 S. Ct. at 2197 (material risk of future harm can suffice "so long as the risk of harm is sufficiently imminent and substantial"); *Susan B. Anthony List v. Driehaus,* 573 U.S. 149, 158 (2014) ("An allegation of future injury may suffice if the threatened injury is 'certainly impending,' *or* there is a 'substantial

14

risk' that the harm will occur.") (emphasis added); *Clapper*, 568 U.S. at 414 n.5; *Massachusetts v. E.P.A.*, 549 U.S. 497, 526 n.23 (2007) ("Even a small probability of injury is sufficient . . . provided of course that the relief sought would, if granted, reduce the probability."); *Deanda v. Becerra*, No. 2:20-CV-092-Z, 2022 WL 17572093, at *2 (N.D. Tex. Dec. 8, 2022) (collecting cases).[14]

For similar reasons, Defendants' reliance on *City of Los Angeles v. Lyons* also fails. 461 U.S. 95 (1983). There, the Supreme Court held Lyons did not have standing to seek injunctive relief because "[t]here was no finding that Lyons faced a real and immediate threat of again being illegally choked" by Los Angeles police. *Id.* at 110. The *Lyons* holding "is based on the obvious proposition that a prospective remedy will provide no relief for an injury that is, and likely will remain, entirely in the past." *Am. Postal Workers Union v. Frank*, 968 F.2d 1373, 1376 (1st Cir. 1992). "No such reluctance, however, is warranted here." *Hernandez v. Cremer*, 913 F.2d 230, 234 (5th Cir. 1990). Considering FDA's 2021 decision to permit "mail-in" chemical abortion, many women and girls will consume mifepristone without physician supervision. And in maternity-care "deserts," women may not have ready access to emergency care. In sum, there are fewer safety restrictions for women and girls today than ever before. Plaintiffs have good reasons to believe their alleged injuries will continue in the future, and possibly with greater frequency than in the past.

---

[14] Defendants' reliance on *Spokeo, Inc. v. Robins* is also unavailing. 578 U.S. 330 (2016). Courts should indeed assess whether the alleged injury to the plaintiff has a "close relationship" to harm "traditionally" recognized as the basis for a lawsuit in American courts. *See TransUnion*, 141 S. Ct. at 2204. But "a plaintiff doesn't need to demonstrate that the level of harm he has suffered would be actionable under a similar, common-law cause of action." *Perez v. McCreary, Veselka, Bragg & Allen, P.C.*, 45 F.4th 816, 822 (5th Cir. 2022). Rather, Plaintiffs only need to show the *type* of harm allegedly suffered "is similar in kind to a type of harm that the common law has recognized as actionable." *Id.*; *see also Campaign Legal Ctr. v. Scott*, 49 F.4th 931, 940 (5th Cir. 2022) (Ho., J, concurring) (evidence of injury required by *TransUnion* is not burdensome). Harm resulting from unsafe drugs is similar to harm actionable under the common law.

Defendants next argue Plaintiffs' theories depend on "unfettered choices made by independent actors not before the courts and whose exercise of broad and legitimate discretion the courts cannot presume either to control or to predict." ECF No. 28 at 20 (quoting *Lujan*, 504 U.S. at 562). "[A] plaintiff must allege personal injury fairly traceable to the defendant's allegedly unlawful conduct and likely to be redressed by the requested relief." *Allen v. Wright*, 468 U.S. 737, 751 (1984), *abrogated on other grounds by Lexmark Int'l, Inc. v. Static Control Components, Inc.*, 572 U.S. 118, 134 (2014); *see also Simon v. E. Ky. Welfare Rts. Org.*, 426 U.S. 26, 41–42 (1976) ("In other words, the 'case or controversy' limitation of Art. III still requires that a federal court act only to redress injury that fairly can be traced to the challenged action of the defendant, and not injury that results from the independent action of some third party not before the court.").

In this case, a favorable decision would likely relieve Plaintiffs of at least some of the injuries allegedly caused by FDA. *See Larson v. Valente*, 456 U.S. 228, 243 n.15 (1982) ("[Plaintiffs] need not show that a favorable decision will relieve [their] *every* injury."); *Duke Power Co. v. Carolina Env't Study Grp., Inc.*, 438 U.S. 59, 74–75 (1978) (a "substantial likelihood" of the requested relief redressing the alleged injury is enough); *Sanchez v. R.G.L.*, 761 F.3d 495, 506 (5th Cir. 2014) (a plaintiff "need only show that a favorable ruling could potentially lessen its injury"); *Texas v. Becerra*, 577 F. Supp. 3d 527, 560 (N.D. Tex. 2021) ("That the plaintiffs have brought forth specific evidence and examples of how they *will* be harmed . . . distinguishes this case from others where a third party's actions *might* have hurt the plaintiff."). And redressability is satisfied even if relief must filter downstream through third parties uncertain to comply with the result, provided the relief would either: (1) remove an obstacle for a nonparty to act in a way favorable to the plaintiff; or (2) influence a nonparty to act in such a way. *See, e.g., Dep't of Com. v. New York*, 139 S. Ct. 2551, 2565–66 (2019) ("[T]hird parties will likely react in predictable ways."); *Bennett v. Spear*, 520 U.S. 154, 169 (1997) (defendants' actions need not be "the very last step in the chain of causation"); *Larson*, 456 U.S. at 242–44; *NiGen Biotech, L.L.C. v. Paxton*, 804 F.3d 389, 396–98 (5th Cir. 2015). Therefore, Plaintiffs' alleged injuries are fairly traceable to Defendants and redressable by a favorable decision.

### 4. *Plaintiffs are within the "Zone of Interests"*

Plaintiffs are also within the zone of interests of the Federal Food, Drug, and Cosmetic Act ("FFDCA") and the Comstock Act. Plaintiffs suing under the APA must assert an interest that is "arguably within the zone of interests to be protected or regulated by the statute that they say was violated." *Texas v. United States*, 809 F.3d 134, 162 (5th Cir. 2015) (internal marks omitted). The zone-of-interests test "is not meant to be especially demanding" and is applied "in keeping with Congress's evident intent when enacting the APA to make agency action presumptively reviewable." *Id.* (internal marks omitted). The zone-of-interests test "looks to the law's substantive provisions to determine what interests (and hence which plaintiffs) are protected." *Simmons v. UBS Fin. Servs., Inc.*, 972 F.3d 664, 669 (5th Cir. 2020). "That interest, at times, may reflect aesthetic, conservational, and recreational as well as economic values." *Ass'n of Data Processing Serv. Orgs., Inc. v. Camp*, 397 U.S. 150, 154 (1970).

A federal court's obligation to hear and decide cases within its jurisdiction is "virtually unflagging." *Lexmark*, 572 U.S. at 126 (internal marks omitted). And "the trend is toward enlargement of the class of people who may protest administrative action." *Camp*, 397 U.S. at 154. No "explicit statutory provision" is necessary to confer standing. *Id.* at 155. "The test forecloses suit only when a plaintiff's interests are so marginally related to or inconsistent with the purposes implicit in the statute that it cannot reasonably be assumed that Congress intended to permit the suit." *Texas v. United States*, 809 F.3d at 162 (internal marks omitted). In other words, "[t]here is no presumption against judicial review and in favor of administrative absolutism unless that purpose is fairly discernible in the statutory scheme." *Camp*, 397 U.S. at 157 (internal marks omitted); *see also Barlow v. Collins*, 397 U.S. 159, 165 (1970) (courts "must decide if Congress has in express or implied terms precluded judicial review or committed the challenged action entirely to administrative discretion").

Defendants argue that Plaintiffs identify no particular provision of the FFDCA protecting their interests. ECF No. 28 at 26. But Plaintiffs' interests are *not* "marginally related" to the purposes implicit in the FFDCA. The statute's substantive provisions protect the safety of physicians' patients and the integrity of the physician-patient relationship. *See generally* 21 U.S.C. § 355. Furthermore, this Court finds Plaintiffs have third-party standing on behalf of their patients. Plaintiffs' patients are within the zone of interest of the FFDCA because patients seek safe and effective medical procedures.

Likewise, Plaintiffs are within the zone of interests of the Comstock Act. This statute "indicates a national policy of discountenancing abortion as inimical to the national life." *Bours v. United States*, 229 F. 960, 964 (7th Cir. 1915); *see also Bolger v. Youngs Drug Prods. Corp.*, 463 U.S. 60, 71 n.19 (1983) (the "thrust" of the Comstock Act was "to prevent the mails from being used to corrupt the public morals"). There is no evidence that Congress "sought to preclude judicial review of administrative rulings" by FDA "as to the legitimate scope of activities" available concerning chemical abortion drugs under these statutes. *Camp*, 397 U.S. at 157. For all the aforementioned reasons, Plaintiffs have standing.

## B. Plaintiffs' Claims Are Reviewable

Defendants aver that "[a]ll of Plaintiffs' claims are untimely or unexhausted except their challenge to FDA's December 16, 2021, response to the 2019 citizen petition." ECF No. 28 at 26.

18

This includes Plaintiffs' challenges to: (1) the 2000 Approval and FDA's 2016 Response to the 2002 Petition challenging that approval; (2) the 2019 Generic Approval; and (3), the April 2021 letter. As for FDA's December 2021 Response to the 2019 Petition, Defendants maintain review is limited to the narrow issues presented in the 2019 Petition — which did not include arguments concerning the Comstock Act. *Id.* at 27–28.[15] The Court disagrees with each of these arguments.

### 1. FDA "Reopened" its Decision in 2016 and 2021

FDA's final decision on a citizen petition constitutes "final agency action" under the APA. 21 C.F.R. § 10.45(c). Challenges to agency actions have a six-year statute of limitations period. *See* 28 U.S.C. § 2401(a). Therefore, the statute of limitations for challenging the 2000 Approval began running on March 29, 2016 — the date of FDA's denial of the 2002 Petition. Because the 2016 Denial of the 2002 Petition occurred more than six years before Plaintiffs filed this suit, Defendants argue the challenge is untimely. ECF No. 28 at 26. But if "the agency opened the issue up anew, and then reexamined and reaffirmed its prior decision," the agency's second action — rather than the original decision — starts the limitations period. *See Texas v. Biden*, 20 F.4th 928, 951 (5th Cir. 2021), *rev'd in part on other grounds*, 142 S. Ct. 2528 (2022).

The reopening doctrine arises "where an agency conducts a rulemaking or adopts a policy on an issue at one time, and then in a later rulemaking restates the policy or otherwise addresses the issue again without altering the original decision."[16] *Wash. All. of Tech. Workers v. U.S. Dep't of Homeland Sec.*, 892 F.3d 332, 345 (D.C. Cir. 2018); *see also Nat'l Biodiesel Bd. v. EPA*, 843 F.3d 1010, 1017 (D.C. Cir. 2016) ("The reopener doctrine allows an otherwise untimely challenge

---

[15] The Court refers to the 2000 Approval, the 2016 Changes and denial of the 2002 Petition, and the 2019 Generic Approval collectively as FDA's "Pre-2021 Actions." Similarly, the Court refers to FDA's April 2021 letter and December 2021 Response as FDA's "2021 Actions."

[16] Courts have even applied the doctrine where agencies decide *not* to engage in rulemaking and then revisit and reaffirm that decision. *See Pub. Citizen v. Nuclear Regul. Comm'n*, 901 F.2d 147, 152 (D.C. Cir. 1990).

to proceed where an agency has — either explicitly or implicitly — undertaken to reexamine its former choice.") (internal marks omitted); *CTIA-Wireless Ass'n v. F.C.C.*, 466 F.3d 105, 112 (D.C. Cir. 2006) (agency "reconsidered" policy by reaffirming policy and offering "two new justifications" not found in prior orders).

In the rulemaking context, courts have identified four non-exhaustive factors to apply the doctrine where the agency: (1) proposed to make some change in the rules or policies; (2) called for comment on new or changed provisions, but at the same time; (3) explained the unchanged, republished portions; and (4) responded to at least one comment aimed at the previously decided issue. *Tripoli Rocketry Ass'n, Inc. v. U.S. Bureau of Alcohol, Tobacco & Firearms*, No. 00CV0273(RBW), 2002 WL 33253171, at *6 (D.D.C. June 24, 2002) (internal marks omitted). But a court "cannot stop there" — it "must look to the entire context of the rulemaking including all relevant proposals and reactions of the agency to determine whether an issue was in fact reopened." *Pub. Citizen*, 901 F.2d at 150. For example, an agency can reopen a prior action if it removes restrictions or safeguards related to the first action or affects a "sea change" in the regulatory scheme. *See Sierra Club v. EPA*, 551 F.3d 1019, 1025 (D.C. Cir. 2008); *Nat'l Biodiesel*, 843 F.3d at 1017 (declining to apply doctrine when "the basic regulatory scheme remain[ed] unchanged"); *Pub. Citizen*, 901 F.2d at 152 (agency reopens decision when it reiterates a policy in such a way as to render the policy "subject to renewed challenge on any substantive grounds").

In the adjudication context, an agency need not solicit or respond to comments to reopen a decision because adjudication does not require notice and comment procedures. *See* 5 U.S.C. §§ 553(c), 554. The reopening doctrine has been applied in the adjudication context where an agency undertakes a "serious, substantive reconsideration" of "a prior administrative decision." *Chenault v. McHugh*, 968 F. Supp. 2d 268, 275 (D.D.C. 2013); *see also Battle v. Sec'y U.S. Dep't of Navy*, 757 Fed. Appx. 172, 175 (3d Cir. 2018) (a petition for reconsideration can restart Section 2401(a)'s limitation period if the agency reopens the action based on a finding of "new evidence" or that the petition reflects some "changed circumstances"); *Peavey v. United States*, 128 F. Supp. 3d 85, 100 (D.D.C. 2015), *aff'd,* No. 15-5290, 2016 WL 4098768 (D.C. Cir. 2016) (reopening in 2011 occurred where agency "elected to conduct a substantive review" of servicemember's 1968 application to correct military records). For formal agency adjudications, even an order stating "only that it is denying reconsideration" is not conclusive if the agency has "altered its original decision." *Sendra Corp. v. Magaw*, 111 F.3d 162, 167 (D.C. Cir. 1997).

The standard for reopening is satisfied here. FDA's requirements for distribution in its 2000 Approval originally included:

- In-person dispensing from the doctor to the patient;

- Secure shipping procedures;

- Tracking system ability;

- Use of authorized distributors and agents; and

- Provision of the drug through direct, confidential physician distribution systems that ensures only qualified physicians will receive the drug for patient dispensing.

*See* ECF No. 1 at 40. FDA's 2016 Changes to this regulatory scheme included the following alterations:

- Extending the maximum gestational age at which a woman or girl can abort her unborn child from 49 days to 70 days;

- Altering the mifepristone dosage from 600 mg to 200 mg, the misoprostol dosage from 400 mcg to 800 mcg, and misoprostol administration from oral to buccal;

- Eliminating the requirement that administration of misoprostol occur in-clinic;

- Broadening the window for misoprostol administration to include a range of 24–48 hours after taking mifepristone, instead of 48 hours afterward;

- Adding a repeat 800 mcg buccal dose of misoprostol in the event of incomplete chemical abortion;

- Removing the requirement for an in-person follow-up examination after an abortion;

- Allowing "healthcare providers" other than physicians to dispense and administer the chemical abortion drugs; and

- Eliminating the requirement for prescribers to report all non-fatal serious adverse events from chemical abortion drugs.

*Id.* at 53–54. And in 2021, FDA removed the "in-person dispensing requirement" and signaled that it will soon allow pharmacies to dispense chemical abortion drugs. *Id.* at 68. Plaintiffs warn that without this requirement, "there is a dramatically reduced chance that the prescriber can confirm pregnancy and gestational age, discover ectopic pregnancies, and identify a victim of abuse or human trafficking being coerced into having a chemical abortion." ECF No. 120 at 19.

FDA's 2016 and 2021 Changes thus significantly departed from the agency's original approval of the abortion regimen. FDA repeatedly altered its original decision by removing safeguards and changing the regulatory scheme for chemical abortion drugs. *Sierra Club*, 551 F.3d at 1025; *Nat'l Biodiesel*, 843 F.3d at 1017. Additionally, FDA's response to the 2019 Petition *explicitly* states FDA "undertook a *full review* of the Mifepristone REMS Program" in 2021. ECF No. 1-44 at 7 (emphasis added);[17] *see also Peavey*, 128 F. Supp. 3d at 100–02 (agency reopened decision by conducting "thorough review" of the merits, even where the order did not state it was a "reconsideration" and did not reference prior decision). And FDA even granted the 2019 Petition in part. ECF No. 1-44 at 3. A "full review" of a REMS for a drug with known serious risks necessarily considers the possibility that a drug is too dangerous to be on the market, any mitigation

---

[17] *See also Questions and Answers on Mifepristone for Medical Termination of Pregnancy Through Ten Weeks Gestation*, FDA (Jan. 4, 2023), https://www.fda.gov/drugs/postmarket-drug-safety-information-patients-and-providers/questions-and-answers-mifepristone-medical-termination-pregnancy-through-ten-weeks-gestation (describing the 2021 review as "comprehensive").

strategy notwithstanding. FDA has the authority to withdraw an approved drug application on this basis. *See* 21 U.S.C. § 355(e). Because the agency reaffirmed its prior actions after undertaking a substantive reconsideration of those actions, the limitations period for those actions starts in 2021. *See Pub. Citizen*, 901 F.2d at 152 (an agency reconsidering and reaffirming original policy "necessarily raises the lawfulness of the original policy, for agencies have an everpresent duty to insure that their actions are lawful").[18]

Alternatively, the Court finds Plaintiffs' claims are not time-barred under the equitable tolling doctrine. *See United States v. Patterson*, 211 F.3d 927, 931 (5th Cir. 2000) (courts "must be cautious not to apply the statute of limitations too harshly"); *P & V Enters. v. U.S. Army Corps of Engr's*, 466 F. Supp. 2d 134, 149 (D.D.C. 2006), *aff'd,* 516 F.3d 1021 (D.C. Cir. 2008) (a "rebuttable presumption of equitable tolling" applies to lawsuits governed by the six-year limitations period of Section 2401(a)); *Bornholdt v. Brady*, 869 F.2d 57, 64 (2d Cir. 1989) ("The existence of § 2401 as a catchall provision . . . does not necessarily mean that Congress intended the six-year period to be applied whenever a substantive statute does not specify a limitations period."). "[A] litigant is entitled to equitable tolling of a statute of limitations only if the litigant establishes two elements: (1) that he has been pursuing his rights diligently, and (2) that some extraordinary circumstance stood in his way and prevented timely filing." *Menominee Indian Tribe of Wis. v. United States*, 577 U.S. 250, 255 (2016) (internal marks omitted); *see also Holland v. Florida*, 560 U.S. 631, 650 (2010) ("The flexibility inherent in equitable procedure enables courts

---

[18] To date, it is unclear whether the reopening doctrine has been applied in the precise context of FDA's approval of an NDA. However, much of the rationale courts have applied in both the rulemaking and adjudication context applies here. And the Court is unaware of any legal principle that would preclude the doctrine from being applied to these facts. Assuming *arguendo* Plaintiffs' allegations are true, a contrary holding would mean there is *no* judicial remedy to FDA's insistence on keeping an unsafe drug on the market, so long as enough time has passed.

to meet new situations that demand equitable intervention, and to accord all the relief necessary to correct particular injustices.") (cleaned up).

Equitable tolling is appropriate here in large part because of FDA's unreasonable delay in responding to Plaintiff's 2002 and 2019 Petitions. *See WildEarth Guardians v. U.S. Dep't of Just.*, 181 F. Supp. 3d 651, 670 (D. Ariz. 2015) (it is "grossly inappropriate" to apply a statute of limitations where the agency unreasonably delayed a claim because the agency "could immunize its allegedly unreasonable delay from judicial review simply by extending that delay for six years") (internal marks omitted). It took FDA 13 years, 7 months, and 9 days to respond to the 2002 Petition. FDA then moved the goalposts by substantially changing the regulatory scheme on the *same day* it issued its Response. And it took FDA 2 years, 8 months, and 17 days to respond to the 2019 Petition which challenged those changes. Thus, in the 20 years between the 2002 Petition and the filing of this suit, Plaintiffs were waiting on FDA for over 16 of those years. *See Hill Dermaceuticals, Inc. v. U.S. Food & Drug Admin.*, 524 F. Supp. 2d 5, 9 (D.D.C. 2007) ("Once citizen petitions are submitted, the FDA Commissioner is required to respond in one of three manners 'within 180 days of receipt of the petition.'") (quoting 21 C.F.R. § 10.30(e)(2)).[19]

Additionally, statutes of limitations "are primarily designed to assure fairness to defendants," and "to promote justice by preventing surprises through the revival of claims that have been allowed to slumber until evidence is lost, memories have faded, and witnesses have disappeared." *Clymore v. United States*, 217 F.3d 370, 376 (5th Cir. 2000), *as corrected on reh'g* (Aug. 24, 2000) (internal marks omitted). But it "has not been argued, and cannot seriously be, that the government was unfairly surprised" when Plaintiffs filed this suit. *Id.* Plaintiffs have been

---

[19] Incidentally, the delayed FDA Response is extreme but not unprecedented. *See, e.g., Bayer HealthCare, LLC v. U.S. Food & Drug Admin.*, 942 F. Supp. 2d 17, 22 (D.D.C. 2013) (FDA had yet to respond to a 2006 petition when it approved a related ANDA in 2013).

reasonably diligent in pursuing their claims. *See, e.g.*, ECF No. 1-4 at 6 (after years of waiting for FDA to respond to the Petition, Plaintiff "called upon" FDA to issue a response in 2005 and again in 2015). And the public interest in this case militates toward resolving Plaintiffs' claims on the merits. Accordingly, Plaintiffs' challenges to FDA's Pre-2021 Actions concerning chemical abortion drugs are not time-barred.

### 2. FDA's April 2021 Decision on In-Person Dispensing Requirements is not "Committed to Agency Discretion by Law"

Defendants also argue any challenge to FDA's decision regarding the in-person dispensing requirement is foreclosed under *Heckler v. Chaney*, 470 U.S. 821, 832 (1985). ECF No. 28 at 30. In *Heckler*, the Supreme Court held that FDA's decision not to recommend civil or criminal enforcement action to prevent violations of the FFDCA was "committed to agency discretion by law." 470 U.S. at 837–38; *see also Texas v. Biden*, 20 F.4th at 982 ("In other words, a litigant may not waltz into court, point his finger, and demand an agency investigate (or sue, or otherwise enforce against) 'that person over there.'"). "[T]he Supreme Court and the Fifth Circuit have consistently read *Heckler* as sheltering one-off nonenforcement decisions rather than decisions to suspend entire statutes." *Texas v. Biden*, 20 F.4th at 983. The "committed to agency discretion by law" exception to judicial review is a "very narrow exception" that applies *only* where "statutes are drawn in such broad terms that in a given case there is no law to apply." *Citizens to Pres. Overton Park, Inc. v. Volpe*, 401 U.S. 402, 410 (1971), *overruled on other grounds by Califano v. Sanders*, 430 U.S. 99 (1977).

That is not the case here. The Secretary has the authority to determine that drugs with "known serious risks" may be dispensed "only in certain health care settings, such as hospitals." *See* 21 U.S.C. § 355-1(f)(3)(C); *Gomperts v. Azar*, No. 1:19-CV-00345-DCN, 2020 WL 3963864, at *1 (D. Idaho July 13, 2020) ("[T]hese restrictions mandate that Mifeprex be dispensed only in certain healthcare settings").[20] The statute also provides other "elements to assure safe use" of dangerous drugs. 21 U.S.C. § 355-1(f)(1), (3). The Secretary must publicly explain "how such elements will mitigate the observed safety risk." 21 U.S.C. § 355-1(f)(2). The Secretary must also consider whether the elements would "be unduly burdensome on patient access to the drug" and must "minimize the burden on the health care delivery system." *Id.* Additionally, the elements "shall include [one] or more goals to mitigate a specific serious risk listed in the labeling of the drug." 21 U.S.C. § 355-1(f)(3). And as the Court will later explain, federal law prohibits the mailing of chemical abortion drugs. Thus, unlike in *Heckler*, there *is* "law to apply" to FDA's decision. *See Texas v. Biden*, 20 F.4th at 982 ("[T]he executive *cannot* look at a statute, recognize that the statute is telling it to enforce the law in a particular way or against a particular entity, and tell Congress to pound sand."). And even if Defendants have significant discretion in how they administer Section 355-1, that does not mean *all* related actions are immune to judicial review under Section 701(a)(2) of the APA.

In sum, Defendants cannot shield their decisions from judicial review merely by characterizing the challenged action as exercising "enforcement discretion." ECF No. 28 at 15; *see also Texas v. Biden*, 20 F.4th at 987 ("The Government is still engaged in enforcement — even if it chooses to do so in a way that ignores the statute. That's obviously not nonenforcement."); *id.* at 985 ("*Heckler* cannot apply to agency actions that qualify as rules under 5 U.S.C. § 551(4)."); *Heckler*, 470 U.S. at 833 n.4 (a decision to consciously and expressly adopt a general policy that is "so extreme as to amount to *abdication* of its statutory responsibilities" is not "committed to agency discretion") (emphasis added). Furthermore, the suggestion that FDA has full discretion

---

[20] *See also Frequently Asked Questions (FAQS) about REMS*, FDA (Jan. 26, 2018), https://www.fda.gov/drugs/risk-evaluation-and-mitigation-strategies-rems/frequently-asked-questions-faqs-about-rems ("A REMS is required to ensure the drug is administered only in a health care facility with personnel trained to manage severe allergic reactions and immediate access to necessary treatments and equipment to managing such events.").

under Section 355-1 to not require *any* REMS for dangerous drugs would likely present nondelegation problems even under a modest view of that doctrine. *See, e.g., Gundy v. United States*, 139 S. Ct. 2116, 2123 (2019). So too the notion that FDA could exercise its non-enforcement discretion in violation of other federal laws. Therefore, FDA's decision to not enforce the in-person dispensing requirement is reviewable because the decision is not committed to agency discretion by law.

### 3. *Plaintiffs' Failure to Exhaust Certain Claims is Excusable*

Plaintiffs allege FDA's 2021 Decision to dispense mifepristone through the mail did not acknowledge or address federal criminal laws that "expressly prohibit[] such downstream distribution." ECF No. 7 at 26. Defendants maintain Plaintiffs' argument is unexhausted because they failed to present it at any stage of any administrative proceeding. ECF No. 28 at 38. Similarly, Plaintiffs have not exhausted their challenge to FDA's approval of the supplemental NDA for generic mifepristone. *Id.* at 26. These failures to exhaust claims do not preclude judicial review.

"The general rule of nonreviewability is not absolute." *Myron v. Martin*, 670 F.2d 49, 52 (5th Cir. 1982). To begin, exhaustion is not required where the agency action is "in excess of" the agency's authority. *Id.* And a court will review for the first time "a particular challenge to an agency's decision which was not raised during the agency proceedings" where the agency action is "likely to result in individual injustice" or is "contrary to an important public policy extending beyond the rights of the individual litigants." *Id.*; *see also Mathews v. Eldridge*, 424 U.S. 319, 330 (1976) ("[C]ases may arise where a claimant's interest in having a particular issue resolved promptly is so great that deference to the agency's judgment is inappropriate."); *Abbott Laboratories v. Gardner*, 387 U.S. 136, 149 (1967) (injunctive remedies applied to administrative determinations should evaluate "both the fitness of the issues for judicial decision and the hardship

27

to the parties of withholding court consideration"); *Dawson Farms, LLC v. Farm Serv. Agency*, 504 F.3d 592, 606 (5th Cir. 2007) (exhaustion may be excused when "irreparable injury will result absent immediate judicial review"); *Bd. of Pub. Instruction of Taylor Cnty., Fla. v. Finch*, 414 F.2d 1068, 1072 (5th Cir. 1969) (exceptional circumstances include "where injustice might otherwise result").

Courts have also excused a claimant's failure to exhaust administrative remedies where exhaustion "would be futile because the administrative agency will clearly reject the claim." *Gulf Restoration Network v. Salazar*, 683 F.3d 158, 176 (5th Cir. 2012) (internal marks omitted); *see also Oregon Nat. Desert Ass'n v. McDaniel*, 751 F. Supp. 2d 1151, 1159 (D. Or. 2011) (exceptional circumstances include evidence of administrative bias). Additionally, courts will consider any issue that was "raised with sufficient clarity to allow the decision maker to understand and rule on the issue raised, whether the issue was considered sua sponte by the agency or was raised by someone other than the petitioning party." *Pac. Choice Seafood Co. v. Ross*, 976 F.3d 932, 942 (9th Cir. 2020). In short, "there is no bright-line standard as to when this requirement has been met." *Nat'l Parks & Conservation Ass'n v. Bureau of Land Mgmt.*, 606 F.3d 1058, 1065 (9th Cir. 2010). Finally, "[a]dministrative remedies that are inadequate need not be exhausted." *Coit Indep. Joint Venture v. Fed. Sav. & Loan Ins. Corp.*, 489 U.S. 561, 587 (1989) (a lack of reasonable time limits in the claims procedure renders the procedure inadequate).

### a.  Contrary to Public Policy

Judicial review of Plaintiffs' unexhausted claims is appropriate for several reasons. First, Defendants' alleged violation of the Comstock Act would be "contrary to an important public policy." *Myron*, 670 F.2d at 52. As a case Defendants rely upon explains, the word "abortion" in the statute "indicates a national policy of discountenancing abortion as inimical to the national life." *See Bours*, 229 F. at 964; ECF No. 28-1 at 206. And twenty-two states filed an amicus brief arguing FDA's decision to permit mail-in chemical abortion harms the public interest by undermining states' ability to enforce laws regulating abortion.[21] ECF No. 100 at 17.

### b. *Individual Injustice and Irreparable Injury*

Second, the agency's actions are "likely to result in individual injustice" or cause "irreparable injury." *Myron*, 670 F.2d at 52; *Dawson*, 504 F.3d at 606. Plaintiffs allege "many intense side effects" and "significant complications requiring medical attention" resulting from Defendants' actions.[22] ECF No. 7 at 13. Many women also experience intense psychological trauma and post-traumatic stress from excessive bleeding and from seeing the remains of their aborted children. *See* ECF No. 96 at 25–29; Pauline Slade et al., *Termination of pregnancy: Patient's perception of care*, J. OF FAMILY PLANNING & REPRODUCTIVE HEALTH CARE Vol. 27, No. 2, 72–77 (2001) ("Seeing the foetus, in general, appears to be a difficult aspect of the medical termination process which can be distressing, bring home the reality of the event and may influence later emotional adaptation."). Parenthetically, said "individual justice" and "irreparable injury" analysis also arguably applies to the unborn humans extinguished by mifepristone — especially in

---

[21] *See* David S. Cohen et al., *Abortion Pills*, 76 STAN. L. REV. 1, 9 (forthcoming 2024) ("Despite state laws, mailed medication abortion can cross borders in ways that undermine state laws . . . A new organization, Mayday Health, for example, focuses on those who live in states with abortion bans, giving users step-by-step instructions on how to set up temporary addresses in an abortion permissive state and forward the mail into the banned state.") (internal marks omitted).

[22] At least 4,213 adverse events from chemical abortion drugs have been reported. *See* ECF No. 96 at 12 n.16. But the actual number is likely far higher because non-fatal adverse events are no longer required to be reported, and because more than 60 percent of women and girls' emergency room visits after chemical abortions are miscoded as miscarriages. *See* James Studnicki et al., *A Post Hoc Exploratory Analysis: Induced Complications Mistaken for Miscarriage in the Emergency Room are a Risk Factor for Hospitalization*, 9 HEALTH SERV. RSCH. MGMT. EPIDEMIOLOGY 1, 1 (2022); *see also* ECF No. 1-8 at 7 (describing Plaintiffs' difficulty in submitting adverse event reports to mifepristone manufacturer Danco). Other data sources such as the Center for Disease Control and Prevention Abortion Surveillance Reports are "profoundly flawed" because state reporting "is voluntary, with many states reporting intermittently and some not at all." Studnicki et al., *supra* note 9, at 2. One Plaintiff physician alleges that when she reported an adverse event to her state's health department, the "report was rejected because the State said it was not a 'true' adverse event because the patient ultimately recovered." ECF No. 1-10 at 7.

the post-*Dobbs* era. *See Dobbs*, 142 S. Ct. at 2261 ("Nothing in the Constitution or in our Nation's legal traditions authorizes the Court to adopt [the] theory of life" that States are *required* "to regard a fetus as lacking even the most basic human right — to live — at least until an arbitrary point in a pregnancy has passed.") (internal marks omitted); Brief of *Amici Curiae* Scholars of Jurisprudence John M. Finnis and Robert P. George in Support of Petitioners, *Dobbs*, 142 S. Ct. 2228 (2022) (arguing unborn humans are constitutional "persons" entitled to equal protection).

### c. Administrative Procedures are Inadequate

Third, FDA's combined response time of over sixteen years to Plaintiffs' two petitions shows their procedures have been inadequate. *See Coit*, 489 U.S. at 587; *Bowen v. City of New York*, 476 U.S. 467, 476 (1986) ("[T]he harm imposed by exhaustion would be irreparable."). FDA slow-walked — or rather, *snail*-walked — its response to the 2002 Petition by waiting nearly *fourteen years* to deny the petition. ECF No. 7 at 9. Requiring Plaintiffs to exhaust their administrative remedies may equate to another decade-plus of waiting for the agency to give them the time of day.

### d. Exhaustion would be Futile

Alternatively, any attempt by Plaintiffs to challenge Defendants' actions would likely be futile. Even if Plaintiffs did not endure sixteen years of delay, dawdle, and dithering, their efforts would surely "be futile because the administrative agency will clearly reject the claim." *Gulf Restoration Network*, 683 F.3d at 176. "President Biden has emphasized the need to protect access to mifepristone" since the day of the Supreme Court's decision in *Dobbs*.[23] President Biden stated that "protecting reproductive rights is essential to our Nation's health, safety, and

---

[23] *See FACT SHEET: President Biden to Sign Memorandum on Ensuring Safe Access to Medication Abortion*, THE WHITE HOUSE (Jan. 22, 2023), https://www.whitehouse.gov/briefing-room/statements-releases/2023/01/22/fact-sheet-president-biden-to-sign-presidential-memorandum-on-ensuring-safe-access-to-medication-abortion/.

progress."[24] He also criticized States' efforts to impose restrictions on mifepristone because such efforts "have stoked confusion, sowed fear, and may prevent patients from accessing safe and effective FDA-approved medication."[25] Thus, it is unlikely FDA would reverse course on its "mail-order" abortion regimen. ECF No. 7 at 7. Defendants' position on the Comstock Act in this litigation only confirms that fact. *See* ECF No. 28 at 38 ("Plaintiffs misconstrue the Comstock Act.").[26]

### e.   The Comstock Act was raised with Sufficient Clarity

Finally, the Comstock Act issue was "raised with sufficient clarity." *Ross*, 976 F.3d at 942. This is because: (1) the 2019 Petition requested FDA to retain the in-person requirement for dispensing of chemical abortion drugs; and (2) the Comstock Act issue was also raised by the United States Postal Service and the Department of Health & Human Services on July 1, 2022, "[i]n the wake of" *Dobbs*.[27] The Office of Legal Counsel specifically mentioned FDA's regimen for chemical abortion drugs when concluding "the mere mailing of such drugs to a particular jurisdiction is an insufficient basis for concluding that the sender intends them to be used unlawfully." OLC Memo at *1. This shows not only that the issue was raised with sufficient clarity, but also the *futility* of raising the issue before the agency. Therefore, Plaintiffs' failure to exhaust their claims does not preclude judicial review.

---

[24] *Memorandum on Further Efforts to Protect Access to Reproductive Healthcare Services*, THE WHITE HOUSE (Jan. 22, 2023), https://www.whitehouse.gov/briefing-room/presidential-actions/2023/01/22/memorandum-on-further-efforts-to-protect-access-to-reproductive-healthcare-services/.

[25] *Id.*

[26] The D.C. Circuit has hinted that the futility doctrine is ordinarily predicated on the "worthlessness of an argument before an agency that *has rejected it* in the *past*" rather than the likelihood that "the agency *would reject it* in the *future*." *Tesoro Refin. & Mktg. Co. v. FERC*, 552 F.3d 868, 874 (D.C. Cir. 2009). But in this case, there is no principled distinction between the two scenarios. Defendants do not even pretend the agency might have accepted Plaintiffs' arguments. Other cases may involve uncertainty about *future* agency rejection, but it is not this case.

[27] *See Application of the Comstock Act to the Mailing of Prescription Drugs That Can Be Used for Abortions*, 2022 WL 18273906 (O.L.C. Dec. 23, 2022) ("OLC Memo").

### C. Plaintiffs' Challenges to FDA's 2021 Actions Have a Substantial Likelihood of Success on the Merits

"To satisfy the first element of likelihood of success on the merits," Plaintiffs "must present a prima facie case but need not show that [they are] certain to win." *Janvey v. Alguire*, 647 F.3d 585, 595–96 (5th Cir. 2011) (internal marks omitted). Under the APA, courts must "hold unlawful and set aside agency action, findings, and conclusions found to be . . . arbitrary, capricious, an abuse of discretion, or otherwise not in accordance with law," or "in excess of statutory jurisdiction, authority, or limitations, or short of statutory right." 5 U.S.C. § 706(2)(A) & (C).

The Court will first address FDA's 2021 Actions that eliminated the in-person dispensing requirement and announced that FDA would allow abortionists to dispense chemical abortion drugs by mail or mail-order pharmacy. Plaintiffs have a substantial likelihood of success on their claims that these actions violate federal law.

#### 1. The Comstock Act prohibits the Mailing of Chemical Abortion Drugs

The Comstock Act declares "[e]very obscene, lewd, lascivious, indecent, filthy or vile article, matter, thing, device, or substance" to be "nonmailable matter" that "shall not be conveyed in the mails or delivered from any post office or by any letter carrier." 18 U.S.C. § 1461. The next clauses declare nonmailable "[e]very article or thing designed, adapted, or intended for producing abortion, or for any indecent or immoral use; and [e]very article, instrument, substance, drug, medicine, or thing which is advertised or described in a manner calculated to lead another to use or apply it for producing abortion, or for any indecent or immoral purpose." *Id.* Similarly, Section 1462 forbids the use of "any express company or other common carrier" to transport chemical abortion drugs "in interstate or foreign commerce."

Defendants' argument that the Comstock Act does not prohibit the mailing of chemical abortion drugs relies on the "reenactment canon." That is, courts may distill a statute's meaning

32

when "federal courts of appeals settled upon a consensus view" and "Congress never modified the relevant statutory text to reject or displace this settled construction." ECF No. 28 at 39. This purported "consensus view" is that the Comstock Act does not prohibit the mailing of items designed to produce abortions "where the sender does not intend them to be used unlawfully." *Id.* This argument is unpersuasive for several reasons.

"Congress is presumed to be aware of an administrative or judicial interpretation of a statute and to adopt that interpretation when it re-enacts a statute without change." *Lorillard v. Pons*, 434 U.S. 575, 580 (1978). But "[t]here is an obvious trump to the reenactment argument": "'[w]here the law is plain, subsequent reenactment does not constitute an adoption of a previous administrative construction.'" *Brown v. Gardner*, 513 U.S. 115, 121 (1994) (quoting *Demarest v. Manspeaker*, 498 U.S. 184, 190 (1991)); *see also Milner v. Dep't of Navy*, 562 U.S. 562, 576 (2011) ("[W]e have no warrant to ignore clear statutory language on the ground that other courts have done so."). Additionally, the presumption only applies when the judicial or administrative gloss "represented settled law when Congress reenacted the [language in question]." *Keene Corp. v. United States*, 508 U.S. 200, 212 (1993); *see also Jama v. Immigr. & Customs Enf't*, 543 U.S. 335, 349 (2005) (presumption applies only when the supposed judicial consensus at the time of reenactment was "so broad and unquestioned that we must presume Congress knew of and endorsed it"); *Davis v. United States*, 495 U.S. 472, 482 (1990); *Fed. Deposit Ins. Corp. v. Phila. Gear Corp.*, 476 U.S. 426, 437 (1986); *United States v. Powell*, 379 U.S. 48, 55 n.13 (1964).[28]

---

[28] *See also* ANTONIN SCALIA & BRYAN A. GARNER, READING LAW: THE INTERPRETATION OF LEGAL TEXTS 325 (2012) ("But how numerous must the lower-court opinions be, or how prominent and long-standing the administrative interpretation, to justify the level of lawyerly reliance that justifies the canon? What about two intermediate-court decisions? (We doubt it — though some cases have relied on just a single intermediate-court decision.) Or seven courts of first instance? (Perhaps.)").

The canon is easily overcome for one simple reason: it is a dubious means of ascertaining congressional intent. "There are plenty of reasons to reenact a statute that have nothing to do with codifying the glosses that courts have already put on the statute." CALEB NELSON, STATUTORY INTERPRETATION 481 (2011). For example, perhaps the original statute contained a "sunset" provision. Maybe Congress wanted to change the statute in some other respects but found it easier to communicate those changes by reenacting a modified version of the complete statute "than by casting each discrete change as an amendment to the existing language." *Id.* at n.14. Or Congress was perhaps conducting "a more general codification or reorganization of the statutes in a particular field, for the sake of making the structure of its statutes easier to follow." *Id.* "Or maybe Congress simply wanted to enact the relevant title of the United States Code into positive law." *Id.* "To the extent that Congress reenacts statutory language for one of those other reasons, members of Congress may well not mean to be expressing any view at all about the glosses that have piled up in the meantime." *Id.*; *see also* HENRY M. HART, JR., & ALBERT M. SACKS, THE LEGAL PROCESS: BASIC PROBLEMS IN THE MAKING AND APPLICATION OF LAW 1367 (William N. Eskridge, Jr., & Philip P. Frickey eds., 1994) (tent. ed. 1958) (criticizing the canon for adding to the costs of the legislative process in counterproductive ways).

Here, the plain text of the Comstock Act controls. *See Bostock v. Clayton Cnty., Ga.*, 140 S. Ct. 1731, 1749 (2020) ("[W]hen the meaning of the statute's terms is plain, our job is at an end."); *Lawson v. FMR LLC*, 571 U.S. 429, 441 (2014) ("Absent any textual qualification, we presume the operative language means what it appears to mean."). The Comstock Act declares "nonmailable" every "article, instrument, substance, drug, medicine, or thing which is advertised or described in a manner calculated to lead another to use it or apply it for producing *abortion*." 18 U.S.C. § 1461 (emphasis added). It is indisputable that chemical abortion drugs are both

34

"drug[s]" and are "for producing abortion." Therefore, federal criminal law declares they are "nonmailable." *See Texas v. Becerra*, No. 5:22-CV-185-H, 2022 WL 3639525, at *26 n.21 (N.D. Tex. Aug. 23, 2022) ("[F]ederal law bar[s] the importation or delivery of any device or medicine designed to produce an abortion.").

The statute plainly does *not* require intent on the part of the seller that the drugs be used "unlawfully." To be sure, the statute does contain a catch-all provision that prohibits the mailing of such things "for producing abortion, *or for any indecent or immoral purpose*." 18 U.S.C. § 1461 (emphasis added). But "or" is "almost always disjunctive." *Encino Motorcars, LLC v. Navarro*, 138 S. Ct. 1134, 1141 (2018) (internal marks omitted). Additionally, the "or" in Section 1461 is preceded by a comma, further disjoining the list of nonmailable matter. Thus, the Court does not read the "or" as an "and." Similarly, the Act requires that the defendant "knowingly uses the mails for the mailing" of anything declared by the Act "to be nonmailable." 18 U.S.C. § 1461. A defendant could satisfy this *mens rea* requirement by mailing mifepristone and knowing it is for producing abortion. The statute does not require anything more. *See, e.g.*, *United States v. Lamott*, 831 F.3d 1153, 1157 (9th Cir. 2016) (where Congress "intends to legislate a specific intent crime," the statute typically uses the phrase "with the intent to") (internal marks omitted).

Even if the statute were ambiguous, the legislative history also supports this interpretation.[29] *See* H.R. Rep. No. 91-1105, at 2 (1970) ("Existing statutes completely prohibit the importation, interstate transportation, and mailing of contraceptive materials, or the mailing of advertisement or information concerning how or where such contraceptives may be obtained or how conception may be prevented."). Congress unsuccessfully tried to modify Section 1461 to

---

[29] This Court reviews the legislative history as mere evidence of the ordinary public meaning of the current statutory language. *See* ANTONIN SCALIA, A MATTER OF INTERPRETATION 17 (1997) ("It is the *law* that governs, not the intent of the lawgiver . . . Men may intend what they will; but it is only the laws that they enact which bind us.").

prohibit mailing drugs "intended by the offender . . . to be used to produce an *illegal* abortion." *See* REP. OF THE SUBCOMM. ON CRIM. JUST., 95TH CONG., REP. ON RECODIFICATION OF FED. CRIM. LAW 40 (Comm. Print 1978) (emphasis added); *Bostock*, 140 S. Ct. at 1824 (Kavanaugh, J., dissenting) ("In the face of the unsuccessful legislative efforts . . . judges may not rewrite the law simply because of their own policy views.").[30] In fact, the House Subcommittee Report on the proposed amendment acknowledged the plain meaning of the statute: "[U]nder current law, the offender commits an offense whenever he 'knowingly' mails any of the designated abortion materials," and the proposed amendment would "require proof that the offender *specifically intended* that the mailed materials be used to produce an illegal abortion."[31] If Congress believed the statute *already* contained the "intentionality" requirement gloss in prior reenactments, there is little reason why Congress would amend the provision to *include* that requirement.

Defendants aver Plaintiffs' interpretation of the Comstock Act is foreclosed by the Food and Drug Administration Amendments Act of 2007 ("FDAAA") for one reason: "Congress was well aware that it was directing mifepristone's preexisting distribution scheme to continue" in enacting the FDAAA. ECF No. 28 at 40. But neither "critics [of FDA's 2000 Approval of mifepristone] nor anyone else in the congressional debate mentioned the Comstock Act." OLC Memo at *7 n.18; *see also In re Lively*, 717 F.3d 406, 410 (5th Cir. 2013) ("Repeals by implication are disfavored and will not be presumed unless the legislature's intent is 'clear and manifest.'") (internal marks omitted). Because the Comstock Act is not even implicitly mentioned

---

[30] *Bostock*'s majority opinion warns that "speculation about why a later Congress declined to adopt new legislation offers a 'particularly dangerous' basis on which to rest an interpretation of an existing law a different and earlier Congress did adopt." 140 S. Ct. at 1747. But the opinion does not suggest judges can "rewrite the law." Instead, *Bostock*'s stated rationale was that the disputed term was implicit in the statutory text all along. No such "textualist" analysis could plausibly justify Defendants' interpretation of the Comstock Act, and Defendants offer none.

[31] REP. OF THE SUBCOMM. ON CRIM. JUST., 95TH CONG., REP. ON RECODIFICATION OF FED. CRIM. LAW 40 (Comm. Print 1978) (emphasis added).

in the FDAAA's enactment, there is no repeal by implication. And in any case, Defendants' arguments based on legislative history cannot overcome clear statutory text.

Consequently, reenactment of the Comstock Act does not constitute an adoption of prior constructions because "the law is plain." *Brown*, 513 U.S. at 121 (1994). Even if that were not the case, the reenactment canon does not apply here because the relevant judicial glosses do not represent a "broad and unquestioned" consensus. *Jama*, 543 U.S. at 349. Defendants rely heavily on the OLC Memo that purports to establish this "consensus." But none of the cases cited in the OLC Memo support the view that the Comstock Act bars the mailing of abortion drugs only when the sender has the specific intent that the drugs be used unlawfully.

On the contrary, the Seventh Circuit reasoned that the word "abortion" in the context of the Act indicates "a national policy of discountenancing abortion as inimical to the national life." *Bours*, 229 F. at 964. *Bours* further declared "it is immaterial what the local statutory definition of abortion is, what acts of abortion are included, or what excluded." *Id.* Similarly, the Sixth Circuit's decision in *Davis v. United States* only suggests that legitimate uses of drugs should not fall within the scope of the statute "merely because they are capable of illegal uses." 62 F.2d 473, 474 (6th Cir. 1933). In other words, the *Davis* holding reflects the position that *legitimate* uses — uses beyond the purposes the statute condemns — should be excluded from the scope of the statute, *not* that whatever uses are *lawful under state law* should be. ECF No. 114 at 10. Likewise, the Second Circuit interpreted the statute to embrace articles the 1873 Congress "would have denounced as immoral if it had understood all the conditions under which they were to be used." *United States v. One Package*, 86 F.2d 737, 739 (2d Cir. 1936). The court further observed that "[t]he word 'unlawful' would make this clear as to articles for producing abortion." *Id.*; *see also* James S. Witherspoon, *Reexamining Roe: Nineteenth-Century Abortion Statutes and the Fourteenth*

*Amendment*, 17 ST. MARY'S L.J. 29, 33 (1985) (explaining that thirty of thirty-seven states had statutory abortion prohibitions in 1868 — just five years before Congress enacted the Comstock Act).

Defendants maintain "the legality of the agency actions needs to be judged at the time of the decision, all of which occurred when *Roe* and *Casey* were still good law." ECF No. 136 at 109. Even assuming that is true in all cases, *Roe* did not prohibit *all* restrictions on abortions. And it is not obvious that enforcement of the Comstock Act post-*Casey* would have necessarily run afoul of *Casey*'s "arbitrary 'undue burden' test." *Dobbs*, 142 S. Ct. at 2266. Therefore, there is no reason why the Act should not have at least been considered. In any case, the Comstock Act plainly forecloses mail-order abortion in the present, and Defendants have stated no present or future intention of complying with the law. Defendants cannot immunize the illegality of their actions by pointing to a small window in the past where those actions might have been legal.

In sum, the reenactment canon is inapplicable here because the law is plain. Even if that were not true, the cases relied on in the OLC Memo do not support Defendants' interpretation. And even if they did, a small handful of cases cannot constitute the "broad and unquestioned" consensus required under the reenactment canon. Therefore, Plaintiffs have a substantial likelihood of prevailing on their claim that Defendants' decision to allow the dispensing of chemical abortion drugs through mail violates unambiguous federal criminal law.

### 2. *FDA's 2021 Actions violate the Administrative Procedure Act*

Because FDA's 2021 Actions violate the Comstock Act, they are "otherwise not in accordance with law." 5 U.S.C. § 706(2)(A). Additionally, the actions were likely "arbitrary and capricious." *Id.* FDA relied on FDA Adverse Event Reporting System data despite the agency's 2016 decision to eliminate the requirement for abortionists to report non-fatal "adverse events."

38

ECF No. 7 at 25. Defendants maintain that "Plaintiffs offer no explanation for why it was impermissible to rely on the reported data." ECF No. 28 at 33. The explanation should be obvious — it is circular and self-serving to practically eliminate an "adverse event" reporting requirement and then point to a low number of "adverse events" as a justification for removing even *more* restrictions than were already omitted in 2000 and 2016. In other words, it is a predetermined conclusion in search of non-data — a database designed to produce a null set. But even if FDA's explanation were well-reasoned, the actions would still run afoul of the Comstock Act and therefore violate the APA.

### D. Plaintiffs' Challenges to FDA's Pre-2021 Actions Have a Substantial Likelihood of Success on the Merits

#### 1. FDA's 2000 Approval violated Subpart H

In 1992, FDA issued regulations "needed to assure safe use" of *new* drugs designed to treat life-threatening diseases like HIV and cancer. *See* 57 Fed. Reg. 58,942, 58,958 (Dec. 11, 1992) (codified at 21 C.F.R. § 314.520). Subpart H — titled "Accelerated Approval of New Drugs for Serious or Life-Threatening Illnesses" — applies to drugs that satisfy two requirements. First, the drug must have been "studied for [its] safety and effectiveness in treating serious or life-threatening illnesses." 21 C.F.R. § 314.500. And second, the drug must "provide [a] meaningful therapeutic benefit to patients over existing treatments." *Id.* "These rules were promulgated by FDA . . . as part of an attempt to correct perceived deficiencies in FDA's approval process made apparent by the need to quickly develop drugs for HIV/AIDS patients." ECF No. 1-13 at 20.

"When FDA originally approved Mifeprex, the agency relied upon Subpart H to place certain restrictions on the manufacturer's distribution of the drug product to assure its safe use." ECF No. 28 at 14; *see also* ECF No. 1-13 at 9 (the American Medical Association explained that "[Mifepristone] poses a severe risk to patients unless the drug is administered as part of a complete

39

treatment plan under the supervision of a physician"). Thus, to satisfy Subpart H, FDA deemed pregnancy a "serious or life-threatening illness[]" and concluded that mifepristone "provide[d] [a] meaningful therapeutic benefit to patients over existing treatments." *See* 21 C.F.R. §§ 314.500; 314.560. FDA was wrong on both counts.

### a. Pregnancy is not an "Illness"

Pregnancy is a normal physiological state most women experience one or more times during their childbearing years — a natural process essential to perpetuating human life. Defendants even admit pregnancy is not an "illness." FDA claims the Final Rule explained Subpart H was available for serious or life-threatening "conditions," whether or not they were understood colloquially to be "illnesses." ECF No. 28 at 36. But the Final Rule says no such thing. "One comment asserted that neither depression nor psychosis is a disease, nor is either one serious or life-threatening." 57 Fed. Reg. 58,946. FDA responded to the comment that "signs of these diseases are readily studied" and that its reference to depression and psychosis "was intended to give examples of conditions or diseases that can be serious for certain populations or in some or all of their phases." *Id.* In other words, FDA's response to this comment was *not* that depression and psychosis qualify because they are "conditions" even though they are not colloquially understood as "illnesses." Rather, FDA simply disagreed with the comment's characterization of these conditions and explained that they *were* examples of "diseases" that can be "serious." Nothing in the Final Rule supports the interpretation that pregnancy is a serious or life-threatening illness.

FDA's 2016 Denial of the 2002 Petition is similarly unpersuasive. For example, FDA noted that approximately fifty percent of pregnancies in the United States are unintended and that unintended pregnancies may cause depression and anxiety. ECF No. 1-28 at 5. But categorizing complications or negative psychological experiences arising *from* pregnancy as "illnesses" is materially different than classifying pregnancy *itself* as a serious or life-threatening illness *per se*. Tellingly, FDA never explains how or why a "condition" would *not* qualify as a "serious or life-threatening illness." Suppose that a woman experiences depression because of lower back pain that inhibits her mobility. Under FDA's reading, a new drug used to treat lower back pain — which can cause depression, just like unplanned pregnancy — could obtain accelerated approval under Subpart H.

Defendants cite zero cases reading Subpart H like FDA reads Subpart H. On the contrary, courts have read "serious or life-threatening illnesses" to mean what it says. *See, e.g.*, *Tummino v. Hamburg*, 936 F. Supp. 2d 162, 182 (E.D.N.Y. 2013) ("Whether an illness is 'serious or life-threatening' 'is based on its impact on such factors as survival, day-to-day functioning, or the likelihood that the disease, if left untreated, will progress from a less severe condition to a more serious one.'") (quoting 57 Fed. Reg. at 13235). The preamble to the final rule also clarified the terms "would be used as FDA has defined them in the past." 57 Fed. Reg. at 13235.

Likewise, the Final Rule expressly stated this nomenclature "is the same as FDA defined and used the terms" in two rulemakings: the first in 1987; the second in 1988. 57 Fed. Reg. at 58,945. In the 1988 rulemaking, FDA defined "life-threatening" to include *diseases or conditions* "where the likelihood of death is high unless the course of the disease is interrupted (*e.g.*, AIDS and cancer), as well as diseases or conditions with potentially fatal outcomes where the end point of clinical trial analysis is survival (*e.g.*, increased survival in persons who have had a stroke or heart attack)." *See* 53 Fed. Reg. at 41517; *id.* at 41516 (referencing "AIDS, cancer, Parkinson's disease, and other serious conditions"); *CSX Transp., Inc. v. Ala. Dep't of Revenue*, 562 U.S. 277, 294 (2011) (the canon of *ejusdem generis* "limits general terms that follow specific ones to matters

41

similar to those specified") (internal marks omitted). Therefore, "diseases" and "conditions" are used interchangeably, and even "conditions" must be "serious" or "life-threatening" as defined.

Food and Drug scholars have understood Subpart H's scope the same way. *See, e.g.,* Charles Steenburg, *The Food and Drug Administration's Use of Postmarketing (Phase IV) Study Requirements: Exception to the Rule?*, 61 FOOD & DRUG L.J. 295, 323 (2006) (Subpart H "extend[s] only to drugs and biological products that target[] 'serious or life-threatening illnesses' and offer[] a 'meaningful' benefit over existing treatments"). Even the Population Council argued to FDA that "the imposition of Subpart H is unlawful" because "[t]he plain meaning of these terms does not comprehend normal, everyday occurrences such as pregnancy and unwanted pregnancy." ECF No. 1-14 at 21. This reading is also consistent with the fact that aside from mifepristone, FDA had approved fewer than forty NDAs under Subpart H by early 2002. *See id.* at 20. And of those *other* approvals, twenty were for the treatment of HIV and HIV-related diseases, nine were for the treatment of various cancers and their symptoms, four were for severe bacterial infections, one was for chronic hypertension, and one was for leprosy. *Id.* "One of these things is not like the others, one of these things just doesn't belong." *See Sesame Street.*

### b. *Defendants are not entitled to* Auer *Deference*

Courts sometimes extend *Auer* deference "to agencies' reasonable readings of genuinely ambiguous regulations." *Kisor v. Wilkie*, 139 S. Ct. 2400, 2408 (2019). *Auer* deference is rooted in an "always rebuttable" presumption "that Congress would generally want the agency to play the primary role in resolving regulatory ambiguities." *Id.* at 2412. "*Auer* deference is sometimes appropriate and sometimes not." *Id.* at 2408. "First and foremost, a court should not afford *Auer* deference unless the regulation is genuinely ambiguous." *Id.* at 2415. "And before concluding that a rule is genuinely ambiguous, a court must exhaust all the traditional tools of construction." *Id.*

(internal marks omitted). "That means a court cannot wave the ambiguity flag just because it found the regulation impenetrable on first read." *Id.* If genuine ambiguity remains, the agency's reading must still be "reasonable." *Id.* And even if the regulation is genuinely ambiguous, the agency's interpretation "must in some way implicate its substantive expertise." *Id.* at 2417. Finally, an agency's reading of a rule must reflect "fair and considered judgment" to receive *Auer* deference. *Id.* (internal marks omitted).

Here, *Auer* deference is not appropriate because "the language of [the] regulation is plain and unambiguous." *McCann v. Unum Provident*, 907 F.3d 130, 144 (3d Cir. 2018). As explained, FDA's definitions in prior rulemakings foreclose its interpretation of Subpart H. If there is any ambiguity in "serious or life-threatening illnesses," the ordinary meaning principle resolves that ambiguity. *See Bostock*, 140 S. Ct. at 1825 (Kavanaugh, J, dissenting) ("The ordinary meaning principle is longstanding and well settled."). "[C]ommon parlance matters in assessing the ordinary meaning" of a statute or regulation "because courts heed how most people would have understood the text." *Id.* at 1828 (internal marks omitted). The word "illness" refers to "poor health; sickness," or "a specific sickness or disease, or an instance of such."[32] Merriam-Webster invokes the definition for "sickness" — "an unhealthy condition of body or mind."[33] Likewise, a Wikipedia search for "illness" re-directs to the entry for "Disease," which is defined as "a particular *abnormal* condition that negatively affects the structure or function of all or part of an organism, and that is not immediately due to any external injury."[34] Pregnancy, on the other

---

[32] *Illness*, Dictionary.com, https://www.dictionary.com/browse/illness (last visited Mar. 22, 2023); *see also Bostock*, 140 S. Ct. at 1766 (Alito, J, dissenting) ("Dictionary definitions are valuable because they are evidence of what people at the time of a statute's enactment would have understood its words to mean.").

[33] *Illness*, Merriam-Webster.com, https://www.merriam-webster.com/dictionary/illness (last visited Mar. 22, 2023).

[34] *Disease*, Wikipedia, https://en.wikipedia.org/wiki/Disease (emphasis added) (last visited Mar. 22, 2023).

hand, is defined as "the time during which one or more offspring develops (gestates) inside a woman's uterus (womb)."[35]

Most readers would not define pregnancy to be a serious or life-threatening illness. Even FDA does not earnestly defend that position. True, complications can arise during pregnancy, and said complications *can* be serious or life-threatening. But that does not make pregnancy *itself* an illness. *See* ECF No 1-13 at 21. And even if the regulation were genuinely ambiguous after exhausting all traditional tools of statutory construction, Defendants' interpretation: (1) is *not* reasonable; (2) does not implicate their substantive expertise; and (3) does not reflect fair and considered judgment. Accordingly, Defendants are not entitled to *Auer* deference on their interpretations of "serious or life-threatening illnesses." By interpreting Subpart H's scope as reaching any state or side effect that can be considered an undefined "condition," Defendants broaden the regulation on accelerated approval of new drugs farther than the text of the regulation would ever suggest. Therefore, FDA's approval of chemical abortion drugs under Subpart H exceeded its authority under the regulation's first requirement.

  *c. Chemical Abortion Drugs do not provide a "Meaningful Therapeutic Benefit"*

FDA also exceeded its authority under the second requirement of Subpart H. In addition to treating a serious or life-threatening illness, chemical abortion drugs must also provide a "meaningful therapeutic benefit" to patients over surgical abortion. 21 C.F.R. § 314.500. As explained, this cannot be the case because chemical abortion drugs do not treat "serious or life-threatening illnesses" — a prerequisite to reaching the second requirement. *Id.* Similarly, chemical abortion drugs cannot be "therapeutic" because the word relates to the treatment or curing of disease.[36] But even putting that aside, chemical abortion drugs do not provide a meaningful

---

[35] *Pregnancy*, Wikipedia, https://en.wikipedia.org/wiki/Pregnancy (last visited Mar. 22, 2023).
[36] *Therapeutic*, Dictionary.com, https://www.dictionary.com/browse/illness (last visited Mar. 28, 2023).

therapeutic benefit over surgical abortion. *See* 21 C.F.R. § 314.500 (examples include where the benefit is the "ability to treat patients unresponsive to, or intolerant of, available therapy, or improved patient response over available therapy"). To the extent surgical abortion can be considered a "therapy," the clinical trials did not compare chemical abortion with surgical abortion to find such a benefit. ECF No. 1 at 44.

Defendants argue just one "meaningful therapeutic benefit": chemical abortion drugs avoided "an invasive surgical procedure and anesthesia in 92 percent of" patients in the trial. ECF No. 28 at 37. But "[b]y defining the 'therapeutic benefit' solely as the avoidance of the current standard of care's delivery mechanism, FDA effectively guarantees that a drug will satisfy this second prong of Subpart H as long as it represents a different method of therapy." ECF No. 1-14 at 22. And even if that *were* a benefit, chemical abortions are over fifty percent more likely than surgical abortion to result in an emergency room visit within thirty days. ECF No. 7 at 21.[37] Consequently, the number of chemical abortion-related emergency room visits increased by over *five hundred percent* between 2002 and 2015. ECF No. 1 at 19.

One study revealed the overall incidence of adverse events is "fourfold higher" in chemical abortions when compared to surgical abortions.[38] Women who underwent chemical abortions also experienced far higher rates of hemorrhaging, incomplete abortion, and unplanned surgical evacuation.[39] Chemical abortion patients "reported significantly higher levels of pain, nausea,

---

[37] Some studies report that the exact number is *fifty-three* percent. *See* Studnicki et al., *supra* note 22.

[38] *See* Maarit Niinimäki et al., *Immediate Complications After Medical Compared with Surgical Termination of Pregnancy*, 114 OBSTETRICS & GYNECOLOGY 795 (2009). FDA agrees with this study but finds it "not surprising" given that chemical abortion "is associated with longer uterine bleeding." ECF No. 1-44 at 38. *See also* ECF No 1-13 at 15, n.68–72 (collecting studies demonstrating the far higher rates of adverse events in chemical abortion over surgical abortion).

[39] *Id.*

vomiting and diarrhea during the actual abortion than did surgical patients . . . Post-abortion pain

occurred in 77.1% of mifepristone patients compared with only 10.5% of surgical patients."

ECF No 1-13 at 24. And before the approval, an FDA medical officer recognized the "medical

regimen had *more* adverse events, particularly bleeding, than did surgical abortion. Failure rates

exceeded those for surgical abortion . . . This is a serious potential disadvantage of the medical

method." *Id.* at 23 (emphasis added).

Other studies show eighty-three percent of women report that chemical abortion "changed"

them — and seventy-seven percent of those women reported a *negative* change.[40] Thirty-

eight percent of women reported issues with anxiety, depression, drug abuse, and suicidal thoughts

because of the chemical abortion.[41] Bleeding from a chemical abortion, unlike surgical abortion,

can last up to several weeks.[42] And the mother seeing the aborted human "appears to be a difficult

aspect of the medical termination process which can be distressing, bring home the reality of the

event and may influence later emotional adaptation."[43] "For example, one woman was surprised

and saddened to see that her aborted baby 'had a head, hands, and legs' with '[d]efined fingers and

toes.'" ECF No. 1 at 21. The entire abortion process takes place within the mother's home, without

physician oversight, potentially leading to undetected ectopic pregnancies, failure of rH factor

incompatibility detection, and misdiagnosis of gestational age — all leading to severe or even fatal

---

[40] *See* Katherine A. Rafferty & Tessa Longbons, *#AbortionChangesYou: A Case Study to Understand the Communicative Tensions in Women's Medication Abortion Narratives*, 36 HEALTH COMM. 1485, 1485–94 (2021), https://www.tandfonline.com/doi/full/10.1080/10410236.2020.1770507.

[41] *Id.*

[42] *After Mifepristone: When bleeding will start and how long will it last?*, WOMEN ON WEB, https://www.womenonweb.org/en/page/484/when-will-you-start-bleeding-and-howlong-will-it-last. *See also* ECF No. 1-28 at 25 ("Up to 8% of all subjects may experience some type of bleeding for 30 days or more.").

[43] Pauline Slade et al., *Termination of Pregnancy: Patient's Perception of Care*, 27 J. OF FAMILY PLANNING & REPRODUCTIVE HEALTH CARE 72, 76 (2001).

consequences. *See* ECF No. 96 at 15–17. Contrary to popular belief and talking points, the evidence shows chemical abortion is *not* "as easy as taking Advil." *Id.* at 20.

Compelling evidence suggests the statistics provided by FDA on the adverse effects of chemical abortion *understate* the negative impact the chemical abortion regimen has on women and girls. When women seek emergency care after receiving the chemical abortion pills, the abortionist that prescribed the drugs is usually *not* the provider to manage the mother's complications.[44] Consequently, the treating physician may not know the adverse event is due to mifepristone. *Id.* at 13. Studies support this conclusion by finding *over sixty percent* of women and girls' emergency room visits after chemical abortions are miscoded as "miscarriages" rather than adverse effects to mifepristone.[45] Simply put, FDA's data are incomplete and potentially misleading, as are the statistics touted by mifepristone advocates.

Lastly, chemical abortion does not "treat patients unresponsive to, or intolerant of, available therapy." *See* 21 C.F.R. § 314.500. "To the contrary, because 'medical abortion failures should be managed with surgical termination' the option for surgical abortion must be available for any Mifeprex patient." ECF No. 1-14 at 23 (quoting the Mifeprex "Warnings" label). One study showed that 18.3 percent of women required surgical intervention after the chemical abortion regimen failed. *Id.* Hence, "any patient who would be intolerant of surgical abortion, if such a class of patients exists, cannot use the Mifeprex Regimen." *Id.* at 24. On balance, the data reflect little to no benefit over surgical abortion — much less a "meaningful therapeutic" benefit.

---

[44] Kathi Aultman et al., *Deaths and Severe Adverse Events after the use of Mifepristone as an Abortifacient from September 2000 to February 2019*, 36 ISSUES IN LAW & MED., 3–26 (2021).

[45] Studnicki et al., *supra* note 9.

*d. Defendants' Misapplication of Subpart H has not been Cured by Congress*

Defendants contend "Plaintiffs' arguments about Subpart H have been overtaken by congressional action." ECF No. 28 at 35. In the FDAAA, "Congress specifically directed" that drugs with elements to assure safe use "in effect on the effective date on this Act" would be "deemed to have in effect an approved" REMS. *Id.* (citing Pub. L. No. 110-85, § 909(b)(1)). But the sponsors of such drugs were also required to submit a proposed REMS within 180 days. *See* Pub. L. No. 110-85, § 909(b)(3). Hence, Congress "deemed" preexisting safety requirements to be a sufficient REMS until a *new* REMS was approved. The FDAAA did not affect, however, whether an NDA was properly approved or authorized under Subpart H in the first place. Rather, the FDAAA required that such drugs needed continued restrictions in place to mitigate risks. Implementation of a REMS under the FDAAA does not somehow repeal or supplant the approval process under Subpart H or 21 U.S.C. § 355(d). The FDAAA only eased the regulatory transition from Subpart H to the REMS provision. Simply stated, Congress's *general* reiteration that dangerous drugs should carry a REMS did not codify FDA's *specific* approval of the mifepristone NDA. It did not consider the chemical abortion approval at all.

In sum, Subpart H doubly forecloses FDA's approval of mifepristone. *At most*, FDA might have lawfully approved mifepristone under Subpart H for cases where a pregnant woman's life or health is in danger. But even a limited approval of this sort would still not render pregnancy an "illness." And surgical abortion — a statistically far safer procedure — would still be available to her. But in any case, that is not what FDA did. Instead, FDA manipulated and misconstrued the text of Subpart H to greenlight elective chemical abortions on a wide scale. Therefore, Plaintiffs have a substantial likelihood of prevailing on their claim that Defendants violated Subpart H.

### 2. *FDA's Pre-2021 Actions were Arbitrary and Capricious*

Under the FFDCA, a pharmaceutical company seeking to market a new drug must first obtain FDA approval via an NDA. *See* 21 U.S.C. § 355(a), (b). The NDA must include "adequate tests by all methods reasonably applicable to show whether or not such drug is safe for use under the conditions prescribed, recommended, or suggested in the proposed labeling thereof." 21 U.S.C. § 355(d). The trials must "provide an adequate basis for physician labeling." 21 C.F.R. § 312.21(c). In those trials, "the drug is used *the way it would be administered when marketed*."[46] The Secretary must deny the NDA if "he has insufficient information to determine whether such drug is safe for use under such conditions." 21 U.S.C. § 355(d)(4).

Here, the U.S. trials FDA relied upon when approving mifepristone required that: (1) each woman receive an ultrasound to confirm gestational age and exclude an ectopic pregnancy;[47] (2) physicians have experience in performing surgical abortions and admitting privileges at medical facilities that provide emergency care; (3) all patients be within one hour of emergency facilities or the facilities of the principal investigator; and (4) women be monitored for four hours to check for adverse events after taking misoprostol. ECF No. 7 at 23. However, FDA included *none* of these requirements — which were explicitly stated in the clinical trial FDA relied on most — in the 2000 Approval. *Id.* Likewise, FDA's 2016 Changes omitted the requirements of the underlying tests: (1) gestational age confirmed by ultrasounds; (2) participants required to return for clinical assessment; and (3) surgical intervention if necessary. *Id.* at 24.

---

[46] *Glossary*, WEILL CORNELL MEDICINE, https://research.weill.cornell.edu/compliance/human-subjects-research/institutional-review-board/glossary-faqs-medical-terms-lay-3 (last visited Mar. 22, 2023) (emphasis added).

[47] The 2016 Denial of the 2002 Petition briefly notes the two French clinical trials did not *require* an ultrasound but instead left the decision to the investigator's discretion. ECF No. 1-28 at 19 n.47. Defendants do not explain how many investigators chose to perform an ultrasound. The higher that number is, the more it supports Plaintiffs' argument. But in any case, the U.S. trial was larger than the two French trials combined and is therefore the more reliable study. *Id.* at 9.

Defendants maintain "there is no legal basis for Plaintiffs' contention that the approved conditions of use of a drug must duplicate the protocol requirements for the clinical trials supporting its approval." ECF No. 28 at 35. But FDA's actions must not be arbitrary and capricious.[48] *See* 5 U.S.C. § 706(2)(A); *United States v. An Article of Device . . . Diapulse*, 768 F.2d 826, 832–33 (7th Cir. 1985) (concluding FDA's denial was not arbitrary and capricious because the proposed labeling did not "specify conditions of use that are similar to those followed in the studies"). "The scope of review under the arbitrary and capricious standard is narrow and a court is not to substitute its judgment for that of the agency." *Motor Vehicle Mfrs. Ass'n of U.S., Inc. v. State Farm Mut. Auto. Ins. Co.*, 463 U.S. 29, 43 (1983) (internal marks omitted). "Nevertheless, the agency must examine the relevant data and articulate a satisfactory explanation for its action including a rational connection between the facts found and the choice made." *Id.* (internal marks omitted); *see also Sw. Elec. Power Co. v. EPA*, 920 F.3d 999, 1013 (5th Cir. 2019) (judicial review of agency action "is not toothless"). Courts must "consider whether the decision was based on a consideration of the relevant factors and whether there has been a clear error of judgment." *Id.* (internal marks omitted). An agency's action is "arbitrary and capricious" if it "entirely failed to consider an important aspect of the problem, offered an explanation for its decision that runs counter to the evidence before the agency, or is so implausible that it could not be ascribed to a difference in view or the product of agency expertise." *Id.* Defendants fail this test.

---

[48] Plaintiffs also frame what the Court characterized as the "study-match problem" as a statutory violation of the FFDCA. *See* ECF No. 7 at 22. The Court does not read 21 U.S.C. § 355(d) as necessarily *requiring* an exact "match" between trial conditions and the conditions on the approved labeling of a new drug. But Section 355(d) does mandate the Secretary "issue an order refusing to approve the application" if he finds the investigations do not show the drug is safe for use under the suggested conditions in the proposed labeling. FDA made such a finding yet did not deny the Application. *See* ECF No. 1-24 at 6 ("We have concluded that adequate information has not been presented to demonstrate that the drug, when marketed in accordance with the terms of distribution proposed, is safe and effective for use as recommended."). Thus, even if Defendants could survive "arbitrary and capricious" analysis of the "study-match problem," Defendants still violated Section 355(d) on their own terms.

### a. The 2000 Approval

To begin, FDA "entirely failed to consider an important aspect of the problem" by omitting any evaluation of the psychological effects of the drug or an evaluation of the long-term medical consequences of the drug. *State Farm*, 463 U.S. at 43; ECF No. 84 at 12. Considering the intense psychological trauma and post-traumatic stress women often experience from chemical abortion, this failure should not be overlooked or understated. Nor was the drug tested for under-18 girls undergoing reproductive development.[49] But that is not all. Clinical trial protocols in the United States for the 2000 Approval required a transvaginal ultrasound for each patient to accurately date pregnancies and identify ectopic pregnancies. ECF No. 1-28 at 19. But FDA ultimately concluded that "a provider can accurately make such a determination by performing a pelvic examination and obtaining a careful history." *Id.* Thus, FDA determined it was inappropriate "to mandate how providers clinically assess women for duration of pregnancy and for ectopic pregnancy." ECF No. 1-28 at 19. FDA believed "it is reasonable to expect that the women's providers would not have prescribed Mifeprex if a pelvic ultrasound examination had clearly identified an ectopic pregnancy." *Id.* at 20.

FDA thus assumes physicians will ascertain gestational age. But put another way, there is simply *no requirement* that *any* procedure is done to rule out an ectopic pregnancy — which *is* a serious and life-threatening situation. This is arbitrary and capricious. The mere fact that other clinical methods can be used to date pregnancies does not support the view that it should be the

---

[49] In 1998, FDA issued the "Pediatric Rule," which "mandated that drug manufacturers evaluate the safety and effectiveness of their products on pediatric patients, absent an applicable exception." *Ass'n of Am. Physicians & Surgeons, Inc. v. U.S. Food & Drug Admin.*, 391 F. Supp. 2d 171, 173–74 (D.D.C. 2005). Two years after approving mifepristone, FDA was enjoined from enforcing the Pediatric Rule because it lacked statutory authority in issuing the rule. *See Ass'n of Am. Physicians & Surgeons v. FDA*, 226 F. Supp. 2d 204, 222 (D.D.C. 2002). In response, Congress enacted the Pediatric Research Equity Act of 2003 to codify the Pediatric Rule. *See* 21 U.S.C. § 355c. In the 2000 Approval, FDA clarified that the Mifeprex NDA was covered by the Pediatric Rule. *See* ECF No. 1-26 at 4. However, FDA fully waived the rule's requirements without explanation. ECF No. 1-28 at 30.

provider's decision to decide which method — if any — is used to make this determination. FDA has never denied that an ultrasound is the *most accurate* method to determine gestational age and identify ectopic pregnancies. *See* ECF No. 1-14 at 62. And the fact that other clinical methods can be used does not mean that all such methods are equal in their accuracy and reliability.[50] FDA did rely on a study showing that clinicians rarely underestimate gestational age. ECF No. 1-28 at 19 n.49. But this study does nothing to support FDA's view that a transvaginal ultrasound is not necessary to diagnose ectopic pregnancies. To this point, FDA merely argues that even transvaginal ultrasounds do not *guarantee* an existing ectopic pregnancy will be identified. *Id.* at 19. If that is the case, it does not follow that it should be left to the provider's discretion to employ less reliable methods — or no methods at all.

Correct diagnosis of gestational age and ectopic pregnancies is vital. The error in FDA's judgment is borne out by myriad stories and studies brought to the Court's attention. One woman alleged she did not receive an ultrasound or any other physical examination before receiving chemical abortion drugs from Planned Parenthood. ECF No. 1 at 22. "The abortionist misdated the baby's gestational age as six weeks, resulting in the at-home delivery of a 'lifeless, fully-formed baby in the toilet,' later determined to be around *30-36 weeks old*." *Id.*; *see also Patel v. State*, 60 N.E.3d 1041, 1043 (Ind. Ct. App. 2016) (woman who used chemical abortion drugs "delivered a live baby of approximately twenty-five to thirty weeks gestation who died shortly after birth"). Another woman was given chemical abortion drugs during an ectopic pregnancy because her ultrasound "was not even that of a uterus but was of a bladder."[51] ECF No. 31 at 5.

---

[50] Studies reflect that women recurrently miscalculate their unborn child's gestational age. *See* P. Taipale & V. Hiilesmaa, *Predicting delivery date by ultrasound and last menstrual period in early gestation*, 97 OBSTETRICS GYN. 189 (2001); David A. Savitz et al., *Comparison of pregnancy dating by last menstrual period, ultrasound scanning, and their combination*, 187 AM. J. OBSTETRICS GYN. 1660 (2002).

[51] This incident also demonstrates that even where ultrasounds are used, only a qualified provider can assure they are done properly.

The resulting rupture "led to massive infection and a collapse of her vital systems." *Id.* Amicus Human Coalition identified four of their clients who were unknowingly ectopic when they arrived at their clinic "with abortion pills in hand." ECF No. 96 at 20. And at least two women died from chemical abortion drugs last year. *See* ECF No. 120 at 30 n.5. One of those women was an estimated twenty-one weeks pregnant. *See id.* Presumably, the fact that the woman obtained chemical abortion drugs more than two months past FDA's gestational age cutoff suggests that no adequate procedures confirmed the gestational age in her case.

FDA has also reported at least ninety-seven cases where women with ectopic pregnancies took mifepristone.[52] But these data are likely incomplete because FDA now only requires reporting on deaths. *See* ECF No. 1 at 4. And as noted above, hospitals often miscode complications from chemical abortions as miscarriages. Studies show that women are thirty percent more likely to die from a ruptured ectopic pregnancy while seeking abortions if the condition remains undiagnosed.[53] A woman may interpret the warning signs of an ectopic pregnancy — cramping and severe bleeding — as side effects of mifepristone. In reality, the symptoms indicate her life is in danger.[54] Another study revealed that of 5,619 chemical abortion visits, 452 patients had a pregnancy of "unknown location" and 31 were treated for ectopic pregnancy — including 4 that were ruptured.[55] Yet another study examined 3,197 unique, U.S.-only adverse event reports dated September 2000

---

[52] FDA, *Mifepristone US. Post-Marketing Adverse Events Summary Through 6/30/2022,* http://www.fda.gov/media/164331/download.

[53] H.K. Atrash et al., *Ectopic pregnancy concurrent with induced abortion: incidence and mortality*, 162 AM. J. OBSTETRICS GYN. 726 (1990).

[54] *Id.*

[55] Alisa B. Goldberg et al., *Mifepristone and Misoprostol for Undesired Pregnancy of Unknown Location*, 139 OBSTETRICS GYN. 771, 775 (2022).

to February 2019.[56] That study noted 20 deaths, 529 life-threatening events, and 1,957 *severe* adverse events before concluding that a pre-abortion ultrasound "should be required to rule out ectopic pregnancy and confirm gestational age."[57]

The record confirms FDA once shared these concerns. After all, many tragedies could be avoided by auditing physician qualifications and requiring ultrasounds. In 1996, the FDA Advisory Committee expressed to the Population Council "serious reservations" on how the drugs were described "in terms of assuring safe and adequate credentialing of providers." ECF No. 1-14 at 51. Population Council initially committed to conducting post-approval studies in 1996, and FDA reiterated these requirements mere months before the September 2000 approval. *See* ECF No. 1-24 at 6 ("We remind you of your commitments dated September 16, 1996, to perform the . . . Phase 4 studies."). Those protocols would have required, *inter alia*, that the Population Council: (1) assess the long-term effects of multiple uses of mifepristone; (2) ascertain the frequency with which women follow the regimen and outcomes of those that do not; (3) study the safety and efficacy of chemical abortion in girls under the age of eighteen; and (4) ascertain the regimen's effects on children born after treatment failure.[58] ECF No. 1-28 at 32.

---

[56] Aultman et al., *supra* note 44.

[57] *Id.*

[58] *See* 153 Cong. Rec. S5765 (daily ed. May 9, 2007) (statement of Sen. Coburn) ("I recently learned of a woman who was given RU-486 after she had a seizure. Her physicians assumed that the seizure was life-threatening to the baby she was carrying and gave her RU-486 for a therapeutic abortion. RU–486 was not effective in her case and the woman carried the baby to term. When the baby was born at a low birth weight, it also suffered from failure to thrive. That baby has had three subsequent brain surgeries due to hydrocephalus. The baby also suffers from [idiopathic lymphocytic colitis] — an inflammatory disease of the colon, which is extremely rare in children. It is clear that RU-486 not only is unsafe in women, but it is also not completely effective. And when it is not effective, the results are devastating.").

Similarly, on February 18, 2000 — months before chemical abortion approval — FDA informed the Population Council that "adequate information ha[d] *not* been presented to demonstrate that the drug, when marketed in accordance with the terms of distribution proposed, is safe and effective for use as recommended." ECF No. 1-24 at 6 (emphasis added). FDA then stated the "restrictions on distribution will need to be amended." *Id.* Accordingly, FDA informed the Population Council that it would proceed under Subpart H — the *only* provision that could implement the requisite restrictions on distribution. *Id.* But as explained above, that was the improper regulation for the approval of chemical abortion. Regardless, the restrictions were insufficient to ensure safe use.

On June 1, 2000, FDA privately delivered to the Population Council a set of proposed restrictions to rectify the safety issues. Said proposal required physicians who were: (1) "trained and authorized by law" to perform surgical abortions; (2) trained in administering mifepristone and treating adverse events; and (3) allowed "continuing access (*e.g.*, admitting privileges) to a medical facility equipped for instrumental pregnancy termination, resuscitation procedures, and blood transfusion at the facility or [one hour's] drive from the treatment facility." *See* ECF No. 1-14 at 53–54. When FDA's proposal was leaked to the press, a political and editorial backlash ensued.[59] In response, the Population Council rejected the proposal and repudiated the restrictions the sponsor *itself* proposed in 1996 — what FDA deemed a "very significant change" in the sponsor's position. *Id.* at 50. Because "[t]he whole idea of mifepristone was to increase access," abortion advocates argued that restrictions on mifepristone "would effectively eliminate" the drug's "main advantage" and would "kill[] the drug."[60]

---

[59] Sheryl Gay Stolberg, *FDA Adds Hurdles in Approval of Abortion Pill*, THE NEW YORK TIMES (June 8, 2000), https://www.nytimes.com/2000/06/08/us/fda-adds-hurdles-in-approval-of-abortion-pill.html.

[60] *Id.*

55

In September 2000, FDA abandoned its safety proposals and acquiesced to the objections of the Population Council and Danco. Despite its "serious reservations" about mifepristone's safety, FDA approved a regimen that relied on a self-certification that a prescribing physician has the *ability* to diagnose ectopic pregnancies. *Id.* at 51, 62; *see also* ECF No. 1-28 at 21 ("[W]e concluded that there was no need for special certification programs or additional restrictions."). FDA later released the applicant *entirely* from its Phase 4 duties — *twelve years* after the 1996 commitment. ECF Nos. 1-24 at 6, 1-28 at 32; *see also* 21 C.F.R. § 314.510 ("Approval under this section will be subject to the requirement that the applicant study the drug further, to verify and describe its clinical benefit, where there is uncertainty . . . of the observed clinical benefit to ultimate outcome. Postmarketing studies would usually be studies *already underway*.") (emphasis added).

FDA *must* refuse to approve a drug if the agency determines there is "insufficient information to determine whether such drug is safe for use" or a "lack of substantial evidence that the drug will have the effect it purports or is represented to have" under the conditions of use in the proposed label. 21 U.S.C. § 355(d)(4)–(5); *see also* 21 C.F.R. § 314.125(b). FDA is therefore required to deny an NDA if it makes the exact findings FDA made in its 2000 review. "[A]n agency's decision to change course may be arbitrary and capricious if the agency ignores or countermands its earlier factual findings without reasoned explanation for doing so." *F.C.C. v. Fox Television Stations, Inc.*, 556 U.S. 502, 537 (2009). The agency must ordinarily "display awareness that it *is* changing position," and "must show that there are good reasons for the new policy." *Id.* at 515. And "if the agency's decision was in any material way influenced by political concerns it should not be upheld." *Earth Island Inst. v. Hogarth*, 494 F.3d 757, 768 (9th Cir. 2007). FDA's only acknowledgments of its prior proposals were that "FDA and the applicant were not always in full agreement about the distribution restrictions" and that fulfilling the Phase 4 commitments "would not be feasible." ECF No. 1-28 at 18, 32–33.

The Court does not second-guess FDA's decision-making lightly. But here, FDA acquiesced on its legitimate safety concerns — in violation of its statutory duty — based on plainly unsound reasoning and studies that did not support its conclusions. There is also evidence indicating FDA faced significant political pressure to forego its proposed safety precautions to better advance the *political* objective of increased "access" to chemical abortion — which was the "whole idea of mifepristone."[61] As President Clinton's Secretary for Health & Human Services ("HHS") explained to the White House, it was *FDA* that arranged the meeting between the French pharmaceutical firm — who owned the mifepristone patent rights — and the eventual drug sponsor Population Council. The purpose of the FDA-organized meeting was "to facilitate an agreement between those parties to work together to test [mifepristone] and file a new drug application." ECF No. 95 at 14. HHS also "initiated" another meeting "to assess how the United States Government" — *i.e.*, the Clinton Administration — "might facilitate successful completion of the negotiations" between the French firm and the American drug sponsor to secure patent rights and eventual FDA approval. *Id.* at 16. In fact, for their "negotiations [to be] successfully concluded," the HHS Secretary believed American pressure on the French firm was necessary.[62] *Id.*

Whether FDA abandoned its proposed restrictions because of political pressure or not, one thing is clear: the lack of restrictions resulted in many deaths and many more severe or life-

---

[61] Stolberg, *supra* note 59.

[62] *See also* Lars Noah, *A Miscarriage in the Drug Approval Process?: Mifepristone Embroils the FDA in Abortion Politics*, 36 WAKE FOREST L. REV. 571, 576 (2001) ("The Clinton administration went to great lengths to bring mifepristone into the United States. From pressuring the hesitant manufacturer to apply for approval, and utilizing a specialized review procedure normally reserved for life-saving drugs, to imposing unusual restrictions on distribution, and promising to keep the identity of the manufacturer a secret, the FDA's approval process deviated from the norm in several respects.").

threatening adverse reactions. Due to FDA's lax reporting requirements, the exact number is not ascertainable. But it is likely far higher than its data indicate for reasons previously mentioned. Whatever the numbers are, they likely would be considerably lower had FDA not acquiesced to the pressure to increase access to chemical abortion at the expense of women's safety. FDA's failure to *insist* on the inclusion of its proposed safety restrictions was not "the product of reasoned decisionmaking." *State Farm*, 463 U.S. at 52. To hold otherwise would be "tantamount to abdicating the judiciary's responsibility under the [APA] to set aside agency actions that are 'arbitrary, capricious, an abuse of discretion, or otherwise not in accordance with law.'" *A.L. Pharma, Inc. v. Shalala*, 62 F.3d 1484, 1491 (D.C. Cir. 1995) (quoting 5 U.S.C. § 706(2)(A)). Finally, the 2000 Approval was also arbitrary and capricious because it violated Subpart H.[63]

b. *The 2016 Changes*

FDA made numerous substantial changes to the chemical abortion regimen in 2016. These changes include but are not limited to: (1) eliminating the requirement for prescribers to report *all* nonfatal serious adverse events; (2) extending the maximum gestational age from 49 days to 70 days; (3) eliminating the requirement that administration of misoprostol occurs in-clinic; (4) removing the requirement for an in-person follow-up exam; and (5) allowing "healthcare providers" other than physicians to dispense chemical abortion drugs. ECF No. 1 at 53–54. Plaintiffs allege the 2016 Changes were also arbitrary and capricious "because *none* of the studies on which FDA relied were designed to evaluate the safety and effectiveness of chemical abortion

---

[63] As one scholar noted, "the agency took this route so that it could better justify imposing otherwise unauthorized restrictions on the use and distribution of the drug." *See* Noah, *supra* note 62, at 582. And "while agency action may generally be 'entitled to a presumption of regularity,' here FDA itself acknowledges that its action has not been regular: it failed to respond to the Citizen Petition for years." *Bayer*, 942 F. Supp. 2d at 25 (internal marks omitted). At the hearing, Defendants' leading argument for Subpart H was that "none of it really matters" because of the FDAAA. *See* ECF No. 136 at 100. "This is not the argument of an agency that is confident in the legality of its actions." ECF No. 100 at 15.

drugs for use under the conditions prescribed, recommended, or suggested in the proposed labeling." ECF No. 7 at 24.

For similar reasons as the 2000 Approval, the Court agrees. Unlike the crucial studies FDA relied upon to extend the maximum gestational age, change the dosing regimen, and authorize a repeat dose of misoprostol, the labeling approved by FDA in 2016 did *not* require: (1) an ultrasound; (2) an in-person follow-up exam; or (3) the ability of abortionists to personally perform a surgical abortion if necessary. *Id.* Simply put, FDA built on its already-suspect 2000 Approval by removing *even more* restrictions related to chemical abortion drugs that were present during the final phase of the investigation. And it did so by relying on studies that included the very conditions FDA refused to adopt.[64] None of the studies compared the safety of the changes against the then-current regimen, nor under the labeled conditions of use. Moreover, FDA shirked any responsibility for the consequences of its actions by eliminating any requirement that non-fatal adverse events be reported. Thus, FDA took its chemical abortion regimen — which had already culminated in *thousands* of adverse events suffered by women and girls — and removed what little restrictions protected these women and girls, systematically ensuring that almost all new adverse events would go unreported or underreported.

Defendants aver that "Plaintiffs point to no statutory provision requiring the conditions of use in a drug's approved labeling to duplicate the protocol requirements used in the studies supporting its approval." ECF No. 28 at 32. "The [FFDCA] thus requires FDA to apply its scientific expertise in determining whether a drug has been shown to be safe and effective under particular conditions of use, and the application of that expertise is owed substantial deference." *Id.* But FDA does not have unfettered discretion to approve dangerous drugs under substantially

---

[64] *See* ECF No. 1-35.

different conditions than the tests, trials, and studies cited. To be clear, the Court does not hold that *any* difference between approval conditions and testing conditions — no matter how well-justified — means the approval fails as a matter of law. But the agency "must cogently explain why it has exercised its discretion in a given manner," and that explanation must be "sufficient to enable [the Court] to conclude that the [agency's action] was the product of reasoned decisionmaking." *A.L. Pharma*, 62 F.3d at 1491 (quoting *State Farm*, 463 U.S. at 52). Defendants have not done so here. FDA's 2016 Actions were not the product of reasoned decision-making.

### c.   *The 2019 Generic Approval*

The FFDCA allows a generic drug manufacturer to submit an ANDA for premarket review and approval. 21 U.S.C. § 355(j); 21 C.F.R. § 314.94. The generic sponsor must show that: (1) the conditions of use prescribed, recommended, or suggested in the labeling have been previously approved; and (2) the drug product is chemically the same as the already approved drug — allowing it to rely on FDA's previous finding of safety and effectiveness for the approved drug. *Id.* On April 11, 2019, FDA approved GenBioPro, Inc.'s ANDA for a generic version of mifepristone. ECF No. 7 at 10. In doing so, FDA relied on Mifeprex's safety data. *Id.*

Plaintiffs argue the 2019 Approval was unlawful because FDA relied on the unlawful 2000 Approval and its unlawful 2016 Changes when approving generic mifepristone. ECF No. 7 at 27. If FDA withdraws the listed drug on which the ANDA-approved generic drug is based, the agency is generally required to withdraw the generic drug as well. 21 U.S.C. § 355(j)(6); 21 C.F.R. § 314.151. Because the Court agrees that Plaintiffs have a substantial likelihood of success in their challenges to the 2000 and 2016 Actions, the Court is inclined to agree with Plaintiffs on this claim as well.

### E. There Is a Substantial Threat of Irreparable Harm

To satisfy the second element of the preliminary injunction standard, Plaintiffs "must demonstrate that if the district court denied the grant of a preliminary injunction, irreparable harm would result." *Janvey*, 647 F.3d at 600 (internal marks omitted). "In general, a harm is irreparable where there is no adequate remedy at law, such as monetary damages." *Id.* (internal marks omitted). "When determining whether injury is irreparable, it is not so much the magnitude but the irreparability that counts." *Texas v. U.S. Env't Prot. Agency*, 829 F.3d 405, 433–34 (5th Cir. 2016) (internal marks omitted). Where "the likelihood of success on the merits is very high, a much smaller quantum of injury will sustain an application for preliminary injunction." *Mova Pharm. Corp. v. Shalala*, 955 F. Supp. 128, 131 (D.D.C. 1997), *aff'd,* 140 F.3d 1060 (D.C. Cir. 1998) (citing *Cuomo v. U.S. Nuclear Regul. Comm'n*, 772 F.2d 972, 974 (D.C.Cir. 1985) (per curiam)). Plaintiffs' Motion satisfies this standard.

For reasons already stated, Plaintiffs are likely to suffer irreparable harm if the Motion is not granted. At least two women died from chemical abortion drugs just last year. *See* ECF No. 120 at 30 n.5;[65] *Deerfield Med. Ctr. v. City of Deerfield Beach*, 661 F.2d 328, 338 (5th Cir. 1981) (finding irreparable harm to third-party pregnant women). "The physical and emotional trauma that chemical abortion inflicts on women and girls cannot be reversed or erased." ECF No. 7 at 28; *see also E.E.O.C. v. Chrysler Corp.*, 733 F.2d 1183, 1186 (6th Cir. 1984) (affirming irreparable harm for plaintiffs' "emotional distress"). "The crucial time that doctors need to treat these injured women and girls cannot be replaced." *Id.* "The mental and monetary costs to these doctors cannot be repaid." *Id.* "And the time, energy and resources that Plaintiff medical associations expend in

---

[65] One of those women was reportedly twenty-one weeks pregnant, which is well past the cutoff for gestational age even after the 2016 Changes. *See id.* The other maternal death occurred while the woman was seven weeks pregnant, which falls within FDA's current restrictions. *Id.*

response to FDA's actions on chemical abortion drugs cannot be recovered." *Id.*; *see also Whitman-Walker Clinic, Inc. v. U.S. Dep't of Health & Hum. Servs.*, 485 F. Supp. 3d 1, 56 (D.D.C. 2020) (obstacles that make it more difficult for an organization to accomplish its mission provide injury for both standing *and* irreparable harm).

Defendants' respond that the drugs at issue have been on the market for more than twenty years. ECF No. 28 at 41. This argument ignores that many restrictions and safeguards — which no longer exist — were in place for most of that time. Defendants also argue "Plaintiffs' extreme delay" in filing suit shows they face no irreparable harm. *Id.* at 42. But the time between the allegedly unlawful actions and the filing of a suit "is not determinative" of whether relief should be granted. *Boire v. Pilot Freight Carriers, Inc.*, 515 F.2d 1185, 1193 (5th Cir. 1975). Here, eleven months does not constitute an "extreme" delay. *See, e.g., Optimus Steel, LLC v. U.S. Army Corps of Eng'rs*, 492 F. Supp. 3d 701, 720 (E.D. Tex. 2020) (eleven-month delay did not militate against equitable relief because "the Court can presume that Plaintiff needed ample time to evaluate its claims").[66] "[T]emporary injunctive relief may still be of great value to protect against ongoing harms, even if the initial harm is in the distant past." *N.L.R.B. v. Hartman & Tyner, Inc.*, 714 F.3d 1244, 1252 (11th Cir. 2013).

The Court also disagrees that Plaintiffs' theories of injury "are too speculative to even show standing." ECF No. 28 at 42. Plaintiffs have credibly alleged past and future harm resulting from the removal of restrictions for chemical abortion drugs. "Although a court's analysis of likelihood of success in the context of an injunctive relief request is governed by the deferential APA's arbitrary and capricious standard, a court does not always owe deference to federal agencies' positions concerning irreparable harm, balance of hardships, or public interest." *San Luis & Delta-*

---

[66] To clarify, the eleven months referenced here is the approximate time between FDA's "final agency action" in the December 2021 Denial of the 2019 Petition and the commencement of this case.

*Mendota Water Auth. v. Jewell*, 969 F. Supp. 2d 1211, 1215 (E.D. Cal. 2013); *see also R.J. Reynolds Vapor Co. v. FDA*, No. 23-60037 (5th Cir. Mar. 23, 2023)[67] (noting FDA's public interest argument was "obviously colored by the FDA's view of the merits"); *Sierra Forest Legacy v. Sherman*, 646 F.3d 1161, 1186 (9th Cir. 2011) ("If the federal government's experts were always entitled to deference concerning the equities of an injunction, substantive relief against federal government policies would be nearly unattainable, as government experts will likely attest that the public interest favors the federal government's preferred policy.").

### F.  Preliminary Injunction Would Serve the Public Interest

The third and fourth factors — assessing the harm to the opposing party and weighing the public interest — "merge when the Government is the opposing party." *Nken v. Holder*, 556 U.S. 418, 435 (2009). "[T]he public interest weighs strongly in favor of preventing unsafe drugs from entering the market." *Hill Dermaceuticals*, 524 F. Supp. 2d at 12. "[T]here is generally no public interest in the perpetuation of unlawful agency action." *State v. Biden*, 10 F.4th 538, 560 (5th Cir. 2021) (internal marks omitted). And "there is a strong public interest in meticulous compliance with the law by public officials." *Fund for Animals, Inc. v. Espy*, 814 F. Supp. 142, 152 (D.D.C. 1993); *see also State v. Biden*, 10 F.4th at 559. "Indeed, the Constitution itself declares a prime public interest that the President and, by necessary inference, his appointees in the Executive Branch 'take Care that the Laws be faithfully executed.'" *Id.* (internal marks omitted). Additionally, Defendants' actions harm States' efforts to regulate chemical abortion "in the interests of life, health, and liberty." ECF No. 100 at 21. "The Court appreciates FDA's institutional interest but, given its long-standing disregard of [Plaintiffs'] Citizen Petition[s], its argument has a hollow center." *Bayer HealthCare*, 942 F. Supp. 2d at 26. To the extent Defendants

---

[67] https://www.ca5.uscourts.gov/opinions/pub/23/23-60037-CV0.pdf.

63

and third parties would be harmed by an injunction, the Court still balances these factors in favor of ensuring that women and girls are protected from unnecessary harm and that Defendants do not disregard federal law.

For these reasons, a preliminary injunction would serve the public interest. Defendants maintain that *unaborted* children of the women "who seek but are unable to obtain an abortion" are "expected to do worse in school," "to have more behavioral and social issues, and ultimately to attain lower levels of completed education." ECF No. 28-2 at 7. "They are also expected to have lower earnings as adults, poorer health, and an increased likelihood of criminal involvement." *Id.* But "[u]sing abortion to promote eugenic goals is morally and prudentially debatable." *Planned Parenthood of Ind. & Ky., Inc. v. Comm'r of Ind. State Dep't of Health*, 917 F.3d 532, 536 (7th Cir. 2018) (Easterbrook, J., dissenting); *see also Box v. Planned Parenthood of Ind. & Ky., Inc.*, 139 S. Ct. 1780, 1790 (2019) (Thomas, J., concurring) ("[A]bortion has proved to be a disturbingly effective tool for implementing the discriminatory preferences that undergird eugenics."). Though eugenics were once fashionable in the Commanding Heights and High Court, they hold less purchase after the conflict, carnage, and casualties of the *last* century revealed the bloody consequences of Social Darwinism practiced by would-be Übermenschen. *Cf. Buck v. Bell*, 274 U.S. 200, 207 (1927) ("It is better for all the world, if instead of waiting to execute degenerate offspring for crime, or to let them starve for their imbecility, society can prevent those who are manifestly unfit from continuing their kind. The principle that sustains compulsory vaccination is broad enough to cover cutting the Fallopian tubes.").

Defendants are correct that one purpose of injunctive relief is to preserve the status quo. *See, e.g., City of Dallas v. Delta Air Lines, Inc.*, 847 F.3d 279, 285 (5th Cir. 2017). But the "status quo" to be restored is "the last peaceable uncontested status existing between the parties before the dispute developed." *Texas v. Biden*, No. 2:21-CV-067-Z, 2022 WL 17718634, at *9 (N.D. Tex. Dec. 15, 2022) (internal marks omitted); *see also Texas v. United States*, 40 F.4th 205, 220 (5th Cir. 2022) (the relevant status quo is the one "absent the unlawful agency action"); *Wages & White Lion*, 16 F.4th at 1144 ("In other words, 'the relief sought here would simply suspend *administrative* alteration of the *status quo*.'") (quoting *Nken*, 556 U.S. at 430 n.1); *Callaway*, 489 F.2d at 576 ("If the currently existing status quo itself is causing one of the parties irreparable injury, it is necessary to alter the situation so as to prevent the injury."). "[P]arties could otherwise have no real opportunity to seek judicial review except at their peril." Mila Sohoni, *The Power to Vacate a Rule*, 88 GEO. WASH. L. REV. 1121, 1157–58 (2020). Chemical abortion is only the status quo insofar as Defendants' unlawful actions and their delay in responding to Plaintiffs' petitions have made it so. The fact that injunctive relief could upset this "status quo" is therefore an insufficient basis to deny injunctive relief.

### G. A Stay Under Section 705 of the APA Is More Appropriate Than Ordering Withdrawal or Suspension of FDA's Approval

The Motion asks for injunctive relief but goes as far as requesting the Court to order Defendants to "withdraw or suspend the approvals of chemical abortion drugs, and remove them from the list of approved drugs." ECF No. 7 at 7. Singular equitable relief is "commonplace" in APA cases and is often "necessary to provide the plaintiffs" with "complete redress." *E. Bay Sanctuary Covenant v. Biden*, 993 F.3d 640, 681 (9th Cir. 2021) (internal marks omitted). Although the Court finds Plaintiffs have a substantial likelihood of prevailing on the merits, the Court instead exercises its authority under the APA to order less drastic relief. Section 705 of the APA provides:

> When an agency finds that justice so requires, it may postpone the effective date of action taken by it, pending judicial review. On such conditions as may be required and to the extent necessary to prevent irreparable injury, the reviewing court, including the court to which a case may be taken on appeal from or on application for certiorari or other writ to a reviewing court, *may issue all necessary and appropriate process to postpone the effective date of an agency action* or to preserve status or rights pending conclusion of the review proceedings.

5 U.S.C. § 705 (emphasis added).

The Fifth Circuit has acknowledged "meaningful differences between an injunction, which is a 'drastic and extraordinary remedy,' and vacatur, which is 'a less drastic remedy.'" *Texas v. Biden*, 2022 WL 17718634 at \*7 (quoting *Texas v. United States*, 40 F.4th at 219). Whereas an injunction "tells someone what to do or not to do," a vacatur only reinstates "the status quo absent the unlawful agency action and neither compels nor restrains further agency decision-making." *Id.* (internal marks omitted). A Section 705 stay can "be seen as an interim or lesser form of vacatur under Section 706." *Id.* "Just as a preliminary injunction is often a precursor to a permanent injunction, a stay under Section 705 can be viewed as a precursor to vacatur under Section 706." *Id.*; *see also Nken*, 556 U.S. at 428–29 (a stay "temporarily suspend[s] the source of authority to act — the order or judgment in question — not by directing an actor's conduct"). "Motions to stay agency action pursuant to [Section 705] are reviewed under the same standards used to evaluate requests for interim injunctive relief." *Id.* at \*10 (citing *Affinity Healthcare Servs., Inc. v. Sebelius*, 720 F. Supp. 2d 12, 15 n.4 (D.D.C. 2010)); *see also Nken*, 556 U.S. at 434; *Texas v. U.S. Env't Prot. Agency*, 829 F.3d at 435. Because the Court finds injunctive relief is generally appropriate, Section 705 plainly authorizes the lesser remedy of issuing "all necessary and appropriate process" to postpone the effective date of the challenged actions. "Courts — including the Supreme Court — routinely stay *already-effective* agency action under Section 705." *Id.* at \*8 (emphasis added) (collecting cases).

66

Accordingly, the Court hereby **STAYS** the effective date of FDA's September 28, 2000, Approval of mifepristone and all subsequent challenged actions related to that approval — *i.e.*, the 2016 Changes, the 2019 Generic Approval, and the 2021 Actions. This Court acknowledges that its decision in *Texas v. Biden* has been appealed to the Fifth Circuit. *See* 2:21-CV-067-Z, ECF No. 184 (Feb. 13, 2023). If the Fifth Circuit reverses this Court's Section 705 analysis, the Court clarifies that it alternatively would have ordered Defendants to suspend the chemical abortion approval and all subsequent challenged actions related to that approval until the Court can render a decision on the merits.

**CONCLUSION**

For the foregoing reasons, the Court **GRANTS** the Motion **IN PART**. FDA's approval of mifepristone is hereby **STAYED**. The Court **STAYS** the applicability of this opinion and order for seven (7) days to allow the federal government time to seek emergency relief from the United States Court of Appeals for the Fifth Circuit.

**SO ORDERED**.

April 7, 2023

MATTHEW J. KACSMARYK
UNITED STATES DISTRICT JUDGE

www.ingramcontent.com/pod-product-compliance
Lightning Source LLC
Chambersburg PA
CBHW051230200326
41519CB00025B/7313